BROKEN CHILDREN,

GROWN-UP PAIN

BROKEN CHILDREN, GROWN-UP PAIN

Understanding the Effects of Your Wounded Past

PAIN

PAUL HEGSTROM

Beacon Hill Press of Kansas City
Kansas City, Missouri

Copyright 2001
by Beacon Hill Press of Kansas City

ISBN 083-411-9102

Printed in the
United States of America

Cover Design: Kevin Williamson

Library of Congress Cataloging-in-Publication Data

Hegstrom, Paul, 1941-
  Broken children, grown-up pain : understanding the effects of your wounded past / Paul Hegstrom.
    p. cm.
  Includes bibliographical references.
  ISBN 0-8341-1910-2 (pbk.)
    1. Adult child abuse victims—Religious life. I. Title.

BV4596.A25 H44 2001
261.8'3273—dc21

                                       2001037624

10   9   8   7   6   5   4   3   2

CONTENTS

For additional information on Life Skills International or any of its affiliate centers, which offer seminars, workshops, training sessions, and personal appearances, interested readers are invited to contact the organization at any of the following addresses and numbers:

Life Skills International
P.O. Box 31227
Aurora, CO 80041

Life Skills International
651 Chambers Rd., Suite 200
Aurora, CO 80011

Telephone: 303-340-0598

Fax: 303-340-0052

E-mail: lsicorp@aol.com

Web site: www.lifeskillsintl.org

ABOUT THE AUTHOR

Paul Hegstrom is founder and developer of Life Skills International, a program designed to teach life skills to individuals with unacceptable behaviors and to enhance family relationships through nurturing character and maturity. Life Skills has grown to over 135 affiliate centers throughout the world and has helped over 70,000 persons since its inception in 1985. Paul holds a bachelor of science degree in pas-

Paul and Judy Hegstrom

toral counseling, is a candidate for a master of science degree in marriage and family therapy, and holds an honorary doctorate from Evangelical Theological Seminary. He is a certified cognitive behavioral therapist with the National Board of Cognitive Behavioral Therapists and has been featured by such national media as *USA Today, Focus on the Family, The 700 Club, Montel Williams, Sally Jessy Raphael,* and *The Coral Ridge Hour.* Paul and Judy Hegstrom's story was featured in the 1995 CBS movie *Unforgivable: The Life Story of Paul Hegstrom,* which starred John Ritter.

✳ ✳ ✳

Paul has compiled a tremendous amount of knowledge, provided by God's common grace, in life span development, brain research, psychology, and systems theory. He has processed that knowledge through Scripture and his personal battle, and he has set forth practical wisdom in plain language. *Broken Children, Grown-up Pain* is of great worth for the clinical professional, pastor, and layperson who want to understand how to bring healing and build godly character in infinitely valuable creatures who have been wounded in this fallen world.

—*Randy Young*
Founding Executive Director
Living Water Counseling/Family Life Skills Ministry
First Church West (Presbyterian Church in America)
Plantation, Florida

ACKNOWLEDGMENTS

I express my heartfelt gratitude to the staff at Beacon Hill Press of Kansas City—especially Bonnie Perry and Jeanette Littleton—and to Mark Littleton and Shannon Hill for their experience in getting this type of book to print.

I also thank my daughter Tammy Smith, who, together with Judy and me, received tremendous healing between a father and a daughter as we revised, discussed, and wept over this manuscript, making this book worth all the effort.

Thank you to all whose lives have been touched by Life Skills International, for your willingness to share your stories as an encouragement to us.

1
OUR STORY

By Paul

Dirty. Damaged. Different.

A ringing echo accompanied the three distinct words my mother used when I, at nine, asked her what would happen if my friend "Tommy" had been molested by an older man. My mother immediately washed my mouth out with soap and reprimanded me for even asking about sex. I wouldn't make that mistake again.

But "Tommy" wasn't the child with the problem. *I* was the one who was "dirty," "damaged," and "different." *I* was the one who had been sexually molested. As a child, I was in no way equipped to deal with my loss of innocence, and I did not know how to cope with those unfamiliar feelings. I immediately lost my sense of safety, my trust in my parents, and every ounce of self-worth a nine-year-old could have. I survived by burying those unpleasant memories. For the next 31 years, the pain from that unresolved incident threatened every aspect of my life: my childhood, my teen years, my relationships, my emotional health, my spiritual condition, my marriage, and every job I had.

As a teenager I grew aggressive and manipulative; yet I maintained a likable personality and became a clown around my friends and family. When I was 13 years old and in junior high on my very first day at a new school, a teacher's assistant asked me to go into the photography class darkroom to develop film. Within minutes, behind closed doors, the teacher's assistant began to molest me. I froze. I was emotionally paralyzed and could not move.

The sexual abuse from that school employee continued for 13 months, during which time I developed a personality that made me feel acceptable to those in my home. Yet within, I had an uncontrollable rage and showed anger while I was at school and with close friends.

My dad was pastor of a large church in the community. Soon he started hearing reports from the parishioners about my fighting, my foul mouth, and my aggressive and hostile behavior at school. They had heard the stories of my behavior from their children, who saw me in action at school. One of the parents went to my mom and told her what I was saying. Because my mom had never seen this side of me, she wouldn't believe the reports. She said, "If Paul were like that, he would slip at home. We would see signs of it."

So I had one personality at school and another "at home" personality that I kept under control. I lived this way for all of my teen years and beyond.

When I was barely 19, I married Judy. I brought home a partner whom I hoped would accept me as I was, including my darker side. The day after our wedding, the cycle of physical and mental abuse began, and it would plague our lives for the next 17 years.

It didn't take me long to realize that I was not prepared for marriage. The responsibilities of having a full-time job, preparing for our first child just days before our first anniversary, and then preparing for our second child just 11 months later were too much for me to handle. I began to run away from the marriage to avoid being an accountable, responsible adult.

I regularly moved from job to job and state to state, sometimes taking Judy and the kids with me. However, I often left them behind for months while I "prepared" for them. Most of the time I was simply running so I could do what I wanted to do without anyone's approval or disapproval.

Internally, I was constantly seeking a fresh start. But a fresh start never happened, because my troubles accompanied me everywhere I went. I began drinking excessively, took recreational drugs, and became involved with numerous women.

I knew something was wrong with me and that counseling didn't have the answers I sought. I recognized my desperation and decided that going into the ministry might help me mature, become accountable, and take care of my family. As a child, I had felt a call into the ministry, and I had been running from that calling for years.

We took our first and only pastorate in a small Midwest town. Before long, some of the children in the church were running home with stories of Pastor Paul arguing with his wife and punching holes in the walls moments before leading the congregation in worship.

I thought the responsibility would stabilize me, but it only made the situation worse.

Disgusted with myself, hating Judy, and apathetic of our kids, I eventually moved them to another location so I could again be free to live as I pleased. I divorced Judy without her knowledge and stopped fighting my impulses. I succumbed to all the anger and rage inside of me.

I eventually began living with another woman. I battered her to the point of facing attempted murder charges with a penalty of 15-22 years in prison.

Loathing all I had done and frightened of a future behind bars, I fell on my knees before God and cried out in pain and despair. I blamed everyone and everything except myself for my problems. I spent close to a year in a recovery program to avoid the attempted murder charge. I spent over $20,000 in private counseling but could not get the help I needed. The program I attended did force me, however, to realize the issues I was dealing with were mine and mine alone. I had emotionally and physically abused every woman in my life. I could not shift the blame any longer.

After hours of arguing with God and justifying my life, my will broke. God spoke to my spirit and told me that I was not teachable but assured me that if I *would* become teachable, He would help me.

The years of rebelling against God had seared my conscience, and I had to begin coming back to God as a child. Through my diligent study using the simplicity of *The Living Bible,* God drew me deeper into His Word and His promises, and my life irrevocably changed. I discovered the truth of who I was and how I had reached bottom. I began to learn that I had reasons—although not excuses—for my years of abusive, controlling behavior. I also realized I was the one all along who needed to change. I had thrown away what I loved the most: my family.

After we had been apart for several years, God brought Judy and me back together. Our reuniting process was slow as we began to develop a friendship—something we had never experienced before. I had damaged her in so many ways that she no longer desired a relationship with anyone, let alone me. Reconciliation was not possible for either of us until God gave us a new love for each other and Judy could learn to trust me again. This would take time and patience.

We were remarried just two days before what would have been our 23rd wedding anniversary, after being separated and divorced for seven years. Our relationship was different from the first time around, and we were growing together as a couple—something new to both of us. Judy started to trust me, although she held some reservation due to the pain that had not yet healed.

Over time our kids discovered I was not controlling and manipulative any longer, and they could see that Judy was truly happy for the first time in her life. All three of our children chose to come home, one at a time.

I was given the tremendous opportunity to start over with my adult children by reparenting them and teaching them what I had learned, and by taking responsibility for all of my past behaviors. I validated their pain, listened to their needs, and shared how much I loved them. This started the healing process in their lives as well.

As our family began healing, the doors of opportunity to share with others in our community opened. As a family, we worked together to build the ministry we now have, which is called Life Skills.

Through the years, as Judy and I have expanded the Life Skills ministry with which God has blessed us, we have learned a great deal about how the traumas of our childhood, if unresolved, manifest themselves in devastating adult behavior. Abuse, hatred, despair, self-loathing, immaturity, irresponsibility, emotional isolation, manipulation, anger, and the inability to bond to a marriage partner are just some of the manifestations of these lasting wounds.

As you continue reading, I would like for you to be aware of some phrases or terms that we will explain further.

Arrested development. The wounds of our childhood hinder our emotional development. We grow physically and chronologically yet remain like children, holding on to our fears and rejection. In adulthood this dynamic makes us feel as if we're crazy, stupid, or defective.

Reactive lifestyles. As we'll see in the following pages, our wounds drive our behaviors. We do not have automatic control of these reactive behaviors, because they're unthinking reactions.

Developmental reconstruction. As we undergo the process of identifying our wounds and recognizing our reactive lifestyles, we'll receive the choice of letting go of the pain and starting to mature. As the apostle Paul stated in Eph. 4:14-15, "Then we will no longer be infants, tossed back and forth by the waves, and blown here and there by every wind of teaching and by the cunning and craftiness of men in their deceitful scheming. Instead, speaking the truth in love, we will in all things grow up into him who is the Head, that is, Christ."

Your life may resemble this type of lifestyle. If so, I want to assure you that God is faithful and you can have hope. As you read, let your mind be open to what God has to reveal to you, and become confident that He has an answer to your pain.

The growing-up process is the development of Christ's character in us.

By Judy

"I now pronounce you man and wife."

Those words rang in my ears, announcing what I thought would be the ultimate in a lifetime of happiness and excitement. Even though my mother had told me, "Life isn't a bowl of cherries," and all the other clichés, I didn't believe her—because my love with Paul was so special that I knew nothing bad could ever happen to us. I had been dreaming of that "knight in shining armor" and the fairy-tale existence. What a deception!

I had grown up in a home with parents who were respected in our church and community. I never imagined the man I would marry would abuse me in every possible way. For all purposes, the word "abuse" wasn't even a part of my vocabulary.

Few young girls imagine a life with the type of person I discovered Paul to be shortly after we were married. Even fewer would envision the years of loneliness, distrust, confusion, hopelessness, and suffering I went through during our first marriage. It became a seemingly endless 17 years of turmoil.

Paul was my husband, I loved him, and he was the father of my children. The abuse made me feel as though I must have given him a reason to hurt me. After repeatedly being blamed for his anger, I began to believe it really *was* my fault and that *I* was the one who needed help, that *I* needed to change.

As a young girl, I thought my home was perfect. During my teenage years, I realized I had a much better rapport with my dad than with my mom and that my brother had a better relationship with my mom than with my dad. I didn't know why, but I felt as if my own mom didn't like me, so I focused more on my dad and my relationship with him. My brother was mean to me. He would lock me in barrels, throw me into swimming pools, sit on me under water, and break things, blaming me each time for whatever happened. My mother would stick up for him, so I began to believe that what I said wasn't heard, let alone important. I believed I didn't matter. I stopped turning to my mom for any comfort or affirmation and turned to my dad, because he would fix my problems, or at least make me feel better. This pattern set me up to readily accept the blame and abuse in my relationship with Paul.

Paul was "the new kid in town." We were both in the same church youth group and soon started a pattern of on-again, off-again dating. I wasn't alarmed at Paul's instability and his need to control me. He was a guy, and that was just how guys were, I figured. My parents never really approved of him and were convinced that he wasn't good enough for their little girl. I felt that my parents were wrong about him, and I was determined to prove them wrong.

In spite of my parents' disapproval, Paul and I were married during my senior year of high school on a Saturday morning in December 1960. The occasion was one of the saddest I've ever faced. Not even I was truly elated with the event. I wanted a real wedding—Paul didn't. Paul wanted his dad to marry us, but his parents were extremely busy, so we had to wedge the event into their time frame. We enjoyed very little planning, had made no arrangements for pictures, and a honeymoon was out of the question.

The day after our wedding, my brother got into an argument with Paul, so I stepped in to stop the fighting. Paul shoved me into a wall. His reaction hurt me physically and emotionally. I began to fear the man I had just married. Was my dad right? I didn't want to hear, "I told you so," so I began to keep the secret.

Behind closed doors, Paul abused me physically, sexually, verbally, and emotionally. I lived under constant threats of abandonment, intimidation, humiliation, and total control. I couldn't open our mail, make phone calls, or have friends, and I had no access to our finances. Paul would come to my workplace and take my paychecks and spend them all. I had to beg for money for personal items or things for the kids. He lied, manipulated, broke all trust, and isolated us again and again. No matter how perfect I tried to be, no matter how obedient I was, I was never good enough for him.

For years Paul moved us from one place to another for his benefit. Three weeks after Paul moved us back up to Minnesota, my daughter asked why I hadn't unpacked the family room full of boxes. I told her I wasn't sure we would be staying and that I didn't feel I even belonged there.

She assured me that everything would be all right this time and encouraged me to grab a box and get started. In one box I thought was mine, I opened an envelope that contained some startling words: "Hegstrom vs. Hegstrom/ Uncontested Divorce."

I went numb and asked myself, "Who is this man? I don't even know who he is."

I could cope with most of his actions, but this was the ultimate blow. I was not about to live with a man when I was not even married to him.

After the initial shock of finding the divorce papers, I was determined to get out on my own and go on with life. I felt the weight of the world on my shoulders. I had to go through the emotional roller coaster and mental anguish of grieving a lost marriage. God got me through thoughts of suicide, depression, major loss of self-esteem, and doubting that He loved women—especially me.

On the other hand, Paul seemed to get by with everything without any consequences. While his family suffered through years of turmoil and abandonment, he was "winning" again. Through all of this turmoil, I still begged God to bring him back so we could start all over again. As I continued praying and time passed, God graciously took away all my feelings for Paul and my desire to have him back. I was able to continue with life without constantly having to deal with the past. Living with Paul had been like opening a fresh wound every day.

Why did I stay with Paul for so long and continue to want him even after all the chaos he brought into our lives. The reasons are complicated, but the information in this book and in our previous book, *Angry Men and the Women Who Love Them,* will help you understand and identify any similar problems in your own life.

When we're in abusive situations, we have to realize that we're not really keeping the secret and hiding the abuse. Often those around us can see the mess in our lives, yet we feel we have it all hidden and under control. We have to come to a stage in which we learn to identify the need, seek the truth, and accept God's grace to guide us into healing.

Paul and I have been remarried now for nearly 18 years. We have been free from any type of abuse this time around.

Day by day we are bonding and working on issues that arise. I continually realize that Paul and our circumstances have changed. Our commitment, combined with a deeper understanding of our pasts, is to build our complete trust in each other. We're all familiar with the time-honored truth that "actions speak louder than words." Trust is earned, proven by time and behavior. This is difficult, but it can happen, and life can be good again—or, as Paul and I have learned as we deal with the past and move forward, life can be better than we ever dreamed possible.

2
"WHY DO I REACT THE WAY I DO?"

John was on trial for murder charges and was facing a possible death penalty. He had reached the bottom when his friend sent him a copy of my first book, *Angry Men and the Women Who Love Them*. John wept as he read it. He had thought he was the only person in the world who was, as he considered himself, "defective." As a result, he had never told anyone else about his background.

As John read on, he could not believe how much the book seemed to describe him. Everything I had written about fit him.

Today John is still in prison, but he now knows a reason exists for his behavior, and he can no longer make excuses. As he connects the wounds of childhood to his adult behaviors, he can grow and develop character no matter what the outcome. This is called *hope*. He didn't understand that what happens to us as children results in lifelong wounds.

The Example of the Oak Tree

What happens in a life like John's in which there's unresolved childhood trauma? I liken it to an oak tree. We can distinguish an oak tree from other trees by the shape of its leaves, the texture of the bark, the measure of shade it provides on a hot day, and even the vivid color of its foliage in autumn. The oak tree is not interchangeable and cannot be confused with a maple, walnut, or evergreen, because each of its characteristics is distinctive.

Likewise, people's traits define their personalities and give depth to their characters. We can dress in whatever's in style this week and make hours of "small talk," but each of us possesses, and is responsible for, his or her individuality. Out of that core person stem the branches of the person's behavior and attitudes.

As adults, we often struggle with unacceptable behavior—such as how we deal with anger, rejection, love, accountability, and authority. As we practice this behavior, we're drawn to others whose behavior is similar to our own, creating a comfort zone. But even in this situation, fear reigns. We wonder what motivates our friends to do and say the things they do, and we fear that they have a personal agenda against us.

When we live in anger and hatred because of our childhood traumas, we grow up to be men and women who are interested only in immediate gratification. Like children, we're self-centered. Like adolescents, we're indecisive and reject authority. We can be dishonest, untrusting, hurtful, controlling, and even abusive.

We may find it impossible to trust others. We doubt everyone's true intentions. We see no reason why anyone would like us. We keep a running list of each past hurt. Then, as is the practice in banking, we "compound interest" on our hurts. We can't heal because we won't let anyone know who we really are. It becomes easier to build walls than to trust others.

We may also be indecisive or feel like a child in an adult body. We may go to extremes—lying, manipulating, controlling, denying, running, and evading issues—to keep ourselves safe. We project a false personality, a mask that conceals the pain driving our anger and fear.

Though we mask our pain, our emotions inevitably surface in our actions. We become emotional pressure cookers as our behavior, attitudes, and anger bleed out in what we perceive as safe, low-risk ways—yet we're never able to resolve the inner turmoil.

An Answer in the Dark

Fortunately, an answer exists. This behavior has a core. It has a reason. A child wounded by rejection, incest, molestation, emotional abuse, or physical abuse will become an adult who is childish in his or her ways. When a child has faced a traumatic experience or cluster of experiences, sometimes he or she never resolves them through forgiveness, growth, or maturing. When left unresolved, such experiences have the power to set a child up for a lifetime of emotional pain and the feeling of being flawed. The emotional development remains at the age and stage of the unresolved trauma. We call this *arrested development.*

What Happens When Development Is Arrested?

The fragile mind of the prepubescent child cannot process and deal properly with significant emotional wounds. Like any other untreated physical wound, the pain deepens and complications develop.

When we reach adulthood, those of us who were wounded as children will not be able to find authentic relationships or build emotional intimacy. We grow chronologically, but our emotions are frozen in childhood. We refuse to believe in a God we can't touch, see, or hear.

The Bible recognizes the consequences of wounding a child. In Matt. 18:6 Jesus says, "Whoever causes one of these little ones who believe in and acknowledge and cleave to Me to stumble and sin [that is, who entices him or hinders him in right conduct or thought], it would be better (more expedient and profitable or advantageous) for him to have a great millstone fastened around his neck and to be sunk in the depth of the sea" (AMP.).

Many of us are dying inside because we can't see a past wound as the source of our adult behaviors. We're powerless and helpless, feeling like children in an adult world. Our abilities to understand our emotions, resolve our conflicts, manage our anger, and cope with our sexuality were stolen from us when we were hurt. Because we're arrested in our development, we can't see the whole picture. We act like children wanting what we want when we want it. This mind-set ushers us into the world of denial. We don't even understand how our pain affects our needs and desires. When we can't identify our issues, we can't address them. We feel powerless and hopeless. We spend the rest of our lives in a survival mode, trying to say alive emotionally and physically. The Bible tells us in Hos. 4:6, "My people are destroyed from lack of knowledge."

As we receive the knowledge and understanding of how we were created, we can be set free from the wounds of a painful childhood.

Five traumas will generally arrest normal development in a prepubescent child: rejection (neglect), incest, molestation, emotional abuse, and physical abuse.

Rejection

Surprisingly, rejection is more damaging to a child than the other four forms of abuse. Rejection occurs in every instance of abuse and acts as an umbrella for the other traumas. It is a subtle destroyer that can take many forms and happen at any stage of childhood. Rejection can include abandonment, a critical spirit, perfectionism, insults, neglect, sarcasm, and even a lack of physical touch.

Sexual Abuse (Incest and Molestation)

When sexual abuse occurs, our value, self-esteem, privacy, and body are compromised. Molestation and incest before puberty tragically and brutally mark the child, because often the abuser is an authority figure, a loved one, or a caregiver. The child's sense of safety is short-circuited and he or she is rendered powerless.

The child's mind doesn't possess the ability to recognize that this is the perpetrator's fault. The child takes responsibility for his or her own trauma, beginning a life of victimization, self-blame, and self-persecution. From this point, the child feels defective.

Emotional Abuse

Emotional abuse is any communication, admonition, or reproof that does not uplift, edify, or bring conflict resolution. It consists of neglect, condemnation, and statements such as "I wish you were never born," "Can't you do anything right?" "You can't be my child," and "You'll never amount to anything." What we've been told as children, combined with how we've been treated, becomes what we believe about ourselves. When we're criticized throughout childhood, the criticism becomes our life commandment. By the time we reach ages eight to nine, those lies become our truth. When criticism comes from our parents, who we assume and believe love us, we again feel defective.

Physical Abuse

Physical abuse is any touch not given in love, respect, and dignity. It emotionally degrades and robs the abused person's value system and self-worth. Distrust and fear spring from the incident, especially if the abuser is a figure of authority or a family member, or if he or she is a trusted person who should have created a safe place of nurturing, caregiving, and protection.

More Than One

Unfortunately, one experience of abuse can set a person up for repeated experiences. Once our self-image is traumatized, we are easily intimidated and can be wounded again and again. I often hear adults ask, "Do I have 'victim' written across my forehead? I keep being hurt again and again."

A feeling of powerlessness takes root after a trauma. "Why couldn't I stop this? What did I do to make that person do this to me?" The anger within the child begins to build, and the child faces feelings of frustration, isolation, and damage.

In nearly all cases of prepubescent abuse, the child finds it extremely difficult to tell anyone what happened. Many times he or she denies the trauma. By being aware of the child's behaviors and moods, we may be able to detect whether or not abuse has occurred or is happening. By encouraging the child to share whatever he or she is thinking or feeling, and always finding a way to affirm the child for these communication efforts, we give him or her a safe place to start the healing process.

Parents, it's vital to tell your children, "Nothing that could happen to you, and nothing you can tell me about yourself, would cause me not to love you." A child needs to know that his or her home is a safe place. The child must know that he or she is loved unconditionally.

The Results of Childhood Trauma

What are the results of these types of trauma? Let me outline several.

Guilt and shame. A child who is unequipped to deal with the emotions attached to trauma will accept responsibility for the incident. "It must have been my fault," becomes the wounded child's battle cry. Later, the weight of the responsibility will result in shame-based behavior. When a child has a shame base, he or she cannot separate his or her value, the value of the person, from the things that happen to him or her. Shame says, "I'm bad. I'm wrong. I'm a mistake. It's my fault."

My son, Jeff, came to me when he was 21 years old and said, "Dad, I wish I had never been born."

"Why would you say that, Jeff?" I asked with surprise.

"Because when our family just consisted of you, mom, Tammy, and Heidi, you all stayed together," he answered. "You and mom didn't divorce until after I was born."

Jeff was an adult at this point but could not release the feeling of responsibility. In his shame, he assumed the blame for his mother and me divorcing.

To carry such feelings of responsibility for years is overwhelming. Therefore, we tend to shift the blame to other people, circumstances, and situations. We have taken responsibility for the harmful incidents of our childhood, and we can't handle additional responsibility.

Guilt is God's way of dealing with the human being. The difference between guilt and shame is that guilt says, "What I *did* was bad, what I *did* was wrong, and I *have* made a mistake. I need to be accountable and take responsibility. When I do, I remain intact, because I know in spite of my mistakes, I have value and can change."

Shame says, "I'm bad. I'm wrong. I'm a mistake. It's my fault."

Shame exists in a system of perfectionism. It leads the child or person to expect rejection, rigidity, isolation, and despair. If I'm living in a shame-based perspective, my perceptions and opinions become my reality. If you question my opinion, you question me.

Guilt exists in a system of accountability, learning, growing, and deepening values. This is the building of a belief system. Fact becomes reality.

Our God-given ability to make choices is the most powerful force in our lives. Shame locks us up; guilt sets us free. We can choose to be set free.

A skewed perspective. Each of us has a unique way of seeing our world. In the beginning of my research 19 years ago, I spent hundreds of dollars on books to pinpoint what "normal" was. After reading and researching for many hours, I realized "normal" was each author's perception—and many of them didn't agree. I then turned to the Bible and began to see an interesting pattern to normalcy and maturity.

During the time when I was so dysfunctional, I thought the world was out of step and I was normal, yet my normalcy was only my perception based upon my fears, lack of maturity, and lack of self-value.

Let's use a simple but effective illustration. I set a cup on a table, and you sit directly across from me. We can see the same cup and agree that it is small, blue, and ceramic. Yet I say the handle is on the left side and you argue that the handle is on the right side. Who's right? We both have different perceptions, yet we're both right.

After a child has been wounded, the abusive incident establishes the child's value from his or her perspective. For example, if a girl is sexually molested, her perception is that her value is based on being a sexual object.

If any wound stems from feelings of abandonment, such as the death of a parent or a divorce, we'll begin to expect people to leave us. We'll conclude that the people who love us will abandon us; therefore, we dare not love.

A child who has suffered rejection will identify others' behaviors as a continuation of that earlier rejection. As an adult, he or she will take comments and actions personally and will look for hidden agendas.

Do you see how one's perspective becomes skewed? We see the cup handle stemming from what seems like different sides, and we're both right—from our point of view. In a healthy mind-set, we can acknowledge that the handle indeed *appears* on both the right or the left, depending on how a person sees it.

However, if we're wounded, our truth depends on how *we* see it. Our perception becomes our reality. When someone disagrees with our perspective, we believe he or she is insulting us or disagreeing with us directly. We think, *If you reject my opinion, you reject me.* We'll fight for our perspectives, no matter how warped they may be.

The cup handle is on the left side, and you're wrong to say anything to the contrary. Our perspective and our self-image as adults has become interwoven through situations and unresolved conflict that occurred in our lives before the age of puberty. As a result, we cannot separate self and perspective in a healthy manner.

We lack trust; we fear truth; we doubt knowledge. At the point of trauma, the child instantly feels powerless and helpless. When the teacher's assistant approached me, my response was to freeze. I felt helpless. "What did I do to cause this?" The security and safety of my childhood world was shattered. When a child faces trauma, a chain reaction is set in motion:

- **Loss of self-respect.** My internal value system has been compromised.
- **Loss of sense of security.** My world is not safe anymore.
- **Lack of trust.** Those I trusted betrayed me. Now I can trust only myself to take care of me.
- **Fear of knowledge.** I fear input, authority, and knowledge because I don't know that it's true. It seems that what you tell me devalues me.

Consciously, you may be aware only of the instant insecurity and fear and the idea that your world is not safe anymore. This now has created your perspective—but it's not reality.

More Consequences

To protect ourselves from more hurt, we

- Collect injustices, keeping a running total of all wrongs against us.
- Develop bitterness. Feeling insecure and defective, we use bitterness to build walls.
- Lash out. This is an active method of pushing people away, fearing they may see that we're defective.
- Fear further rejection. We expend a lot of energy to keep from being rejected. We will even criticize ourselves to diffuse the situation so others can't hurt us. Fearing rejection, we isolate ourselves. Isolation is lonely, but we've now established a self-protection plan.

The Blame Game

We don't need to delve into our past and search for a specific trauma that may have caused lasting results. What's relevant is that we identify our behaviors and emotions and realize that they have a source. What we identify and can understand, we can deal with; but what we can't identify and don't understand drives us crazy.

Unacceptable behaviors such as anger and rage don't come out of a vacuum. There's always a source. But in confronting our pain, we may be tempted to look at those responsible for our lack of security in childhood or to blame those who trigger our behaviors. We begin blaming everyone but ourselves for our problems. This book is not written to blame parents or others, but rather to move us to identify and take responsibility for our childish, unacceptable behavior. Always remember that our recovery is not tied to our parents' response. I want to help you stop playing the blame game by accepting responsibility for your behavior today.

A parent who doesn't know that his or her child has

been traumatized can't help the child deal properly with the trauma. At times, the child will have suffered a damaging experience and does not have the ability to explain exactly what happened and how it hurts. How often do toddlers hurt themselves yet are completely helpless in expressing what happened? A mother or father will try to comfort an angry, frustrated, crying child by rocking and making soothing sounds—without knowing the details of the upsetting situation.

As adults, we may exhibit the same behaviors we did as children, hoping to find comfort. We may have the feelings of being hurt but can't put our feelings into words.

Many times traumas happen outside of the family unit, and the family does not know the child has been wounded. This is not the parents' fault. It would be pointless to accuse our parents or caregivers of not giving us the tools to deal with our wounds. When we look at our families, often we'll discover that our parents have never dealt with their own pain and therefore cannot recognize the severity of our wounds and their effect upon us.

Too often, however, the trauma comes from within the family unit, and the parents *are* responsible for wounding the child. We can't change the past, and we can't change our parents. But we *can* break the cycle of blaming others and choose to start the process of emotional healing.

My mother's father beat her savagely with a board when she was eight years old, causing permanent physical damage. She was never able to forgive him. I first heard this story when she was 83 years old. This incident of physical abuse began a lifetime of reactions. When she realized much of her emotional pain was rooted in that experience as an eight-year-old, she was freed from the responsibility of what her father had done. She then forgave him, and her life has changed dramatically.

Denial

Another reaction to childhood trauma is denial. Little children will cover their eyes and ears when they don't want to see or hear something unpleasant. Denial is our

Creator's gift to us to keep us alive until someone we can learn to trust can make sense of life. Denial provides the perception of a safe haven until we have the right guidance to make sense of what we feel.

The feeling of something being wrong with us is part of our perspective as well. We have difficulty recognizing that many people suffer as we do. People who are angry, distrustful, personally irresponsible, and hateful of authority trigger us, and we personalize their pain, thus creating even more anger within ourselves.

Frequently, a couple will come in for counseling, and I see that both persons are wounded—they're angry at themselves and each other. They deny their own issues and blame the other person. Often they think the other person has a hidden agenda.

I believe that by looking at the way God designed us to grow to maturity, we can become confident that we're not defective. We also can realize that what occurred to us in our childhood was not our fault or responsibility; therefore, we don't have to take the blame or responsibility for it any longer—although we must claim responsibility for our behavior as an adult.

Ultimately, the wounds of childhood, which arrest our development, amplify the sin nature, and we become *childish*. Christ called us in Matt. 18:4 to become *childlike*, "trusting, lowly, loving, forgiving," and not *childish* (AMP).

When we seek wholeness and healing from the wounds of our past, we can begin to give up the traits, habits, and undeveloped character we cling to and restart our growth by developing the character of Christ.

This is the first step toward overcoming the problem of arrested development.

THE WAY
WE'RE WIRED

"I was just born that way."

Have you ever heard someone utter this popular excuse? It's really a dangerous myth. The person who believes it will feel discouraged by his or her behavior and emotions, trapped by the idea that he or she was "just born that way." Such people are certain that in the plan of the universe, they were destined to draw the short stick.

By looking at the way God intended our biological, spiritual, emotional, and social development to work together, we can see that we're not unbalanced because we face frustration and character flaws. In spite of our sin nature, God's ways bring us wholeness if we have a teachable spirit.

The Physiology

Before the age of puberty, children lack a significant presence of three important chemicals in their brains: serotonin, dopamine, and norepinephrine. The combination of these chemicals is not released in the brain of a child until the pituitary gland triggers the child into puberty at eight-and-a-half to nine years of age. When the pituitary gland releases the growth hormones, the chemical structure of the child starts to change. The physical body begins to transform; boys and girls become young men and women. However, the physical and mental changes may not be apparent until the ages of 11 to 15.

As the body develops, the brain begins to function in a new way. The child grows from thinking only concretely to developing the abstract thinking process of an adult. This process prepares teenagers to begin making their own decisions. The prepubescent child has little reasoning ability. The chemical change provides the child with the ability to become a decision maker for a lifetime.

As the apostle Paul tells us in 1 Cor. 13:11: "When I was a child, I spoke as a child, I understood as a child, I thought as a child; but when I became a man, I put away childish things" (NKJV).

This scripture motivated me to research how children think and reason differently than adults. I realized that I had thought and reasoned like a child for 40 years. Because of this verse, I felt tremendous hope that I could emotionally "grow up," because Paul was writing this to adults, not to children.

Look at a group of children playing with a ball. The ball rolls into the street. They'll naturally be tempted to chase after the ball without thinking about oncoming traffic or other consequences. Adults, however, recognize the danger. By processing how fast the ball is moving and the speed and location of the traffic, they can calculate the best opportunity to retrieve the ball. The children just want to start playing again, so they will want only to retrieve the ball, unaware of any danger or consequence.

The young child learns by boundaries, directives, and either positive consequences for obedience or negative consequences for disobedience. The consistency of the training creates a lifelong pattern in the child. The mind is like a programmed computer—I believe God designed the human brain as the most magnificent computer on earth, ready to receive and process information, data, and experiences.

We can compare our five senses to a keyboard that feeds information into the "hard drive" of our brain. In this hard drive, God created a "program" with proper information that will bring us to a healthy and meaningful relationship with Him and others. As with all good computer programs that we can load onto our personal computers, we have a user's manual. God gave us our instruction manual in the Bible (See Isa. 28:9-10).

The Computer

In the mating process, chromosomes collide, and the DNA helix is built. This creates in the woman's womb an entirely new person with a unique personality. As the brain is formed, certain truths remain the same for each of us if we're blessed to be born healthy and whole. In Ps. 139:13-16, the psalmist shares that God knew us before we were formed and before the foundation of the world was made.

Looking at the brain as if it were wired as a computer, we see that everything happens on a very small but powerful scale. If we could replicate the human brain in the form of a computer, it would take the capacity of 750 billion mainframes linked together. Housing this size of computer would take a building 100 stories tall and the size of Texas. Our Creator has the tremendous ability to miniaturize, as our brain weighs an average of three pounds.

The brain is constructed of billions of neurons and synapses. Each neuron is a thinking pathway, and its connections are bathed in chemicals. As we mature and this wiring develops, the chemicals surrounding each neuron act as insulation to protect our thinking processes. When we make a conscious choice to change, new wiring is required and automatically developed by the persistence of our will and choice.

However, if we've been immersed in negative, traumatic experiences, those experiences become wired into our brains, just like any other situation. Like stubborn and complicated personal computers, we become "conformed" to our original system and the old wiring that incorporates those traumas resists changing.

This is where our will becomes a change maker. If we decide to change despite our trauma, we must override the old wiring with our God-given free will. The Bible encourages us to do this in Rom. 12:2—"Do not be conformed to this world, but be transformed by the renewing of your mind, that you may prove what is that good and acceptable and perfect will of God" (NKJV).

The Software

Any computer is only as good as the software that runs it. Without the software, your desktop or laptop is only molded plastic and wires.

The same is true of your brain. It is a powerful computer, but only useful if the software is in place to promote your growth and development—mentally, emotionally, spiritually, and physically. In the "software" we use to run our thoughts lies the basis for normalcy. Our software is programmed so there is a time and place for certain things to happen in life.

In our Life Skills program, we've discovered that psychological researcher Erik Erickson's Life Span Development Model supports the biblical approach to growth. Both the scripture and Erickson's model reveal eight life stages from birth to maturity. For example, the software of the brain tells us that all sexuality should have a foundation of emotional intimacy and marriage before physical intimacy can begin. Many people have ignored this principle and have had sex outside of marriage. Thus, they ignore this foundational programming based on the wide acceptance of casual sex. This collides with God's "wiring" and our normal internal software. If we ignore the requirements of emotional bonding and marriage for sexuality, our ability to maintain intimacy is irrevocably altered.

Mothering is built into the programming of a woman. That doesn't mean that all women are instantly great mothers or that all must have children. Yet at the right point in her individual maturing, a woman will naturally know how to respond to a child's cry for food, attention, and love. As part of her internal software, she is prepared to care for her child.

The cases of murder or abuse that incense the public most are usually those of mothers who have turned against their children. These crimes feel intensely *unnatural* because each of us knows through our software that our Creator intended something entirely different.

The Documentation

God planned the software and wrote the manual to show us how to use it. What is that manual? The Bible.

The Creator provided an "owner's manual" for this intricately designed computer system and software called human personality. Solely standing on the basis of historical documentation, critics will agree that the Bible offers an excellent structure for social interaction.

Bringing It All Together

How does this relate to our principle of arrested development?

When a child is wounded emotionally, his or her whole life is colored by that trauma. The child cannot reason or see reality. Without the structure to reason, the child automatically thinks, *What did I do to cause this grown-up to do this to me?*

As the child grows, the unresolved trauma locks him or her into a survival mode. The child's emotional development is halted, and he or she develops survival techniques instead of changing.

My wife, Judy, who had suffered her own trauma as a child, stayed in our abusive marriage for nearly 17 years. She had never developed those reasoning processes and could not reason that I was at fault. As with her early experiences with her mother and brother, she constantly questioned what she had done to deserve the abuse. Because she was convinced she was to blame, she desperately tried to change to appease me.

An Ancient Custom

Biology isn't the only evidence we are given that arrested development was not God's design for full living. Looking at the Bible and Jewish culture, we see a blueprint of the development of young men and women, trained and nurtured to become valuable additions to their community.

The years from birth to age 13 are considered the age of directives for a young person raised in the Jewish tradition. During this period, the parents and the extended family teach the child responsibility, accountability, respect, and a faith-based foundation. This upbringing prepares the child to move into adolescence, marked at the age of 13 by the boy's bar mitzvah and the girl's bat mitzvah at age 12.

The bar mitzvah ceremony is crucial in the young man's life. The rabbi proclaims this rite of passage as a momentous day of celebration, because the child is moving into the age of decision. The rabbi explains, "From now on, son, you will be responsible for the consequences of your behavior and your decisions."

The rabbi then congratulates the parents for teaching their son how to build relationships and take responsibility for his actions. At one point in the ceremony, the father kneels, raises his hands toward heaven, and repeats after the rabbi, "Jehovah, I thank you for releasing me from the responsibility of the consequences of this child's decisions and behavior."

What a great day in any dad's life!

In the Jewish culture, the child then moves into adolescence and the age of decision, during which he will learn under the tutelage of the older family members for the next 17 years. This is called "the age of parental management." The young man may marry, but he will still work and train with his older brothers, father, grandfathers, and uncles. He will make decisions but will use the elders of the family as wise counsel. If he makes a mistake as he's learning to make a good decision, the extended family helps him deal with that mistake. When a young man reaches 30 years of age, he enters "full stature" or "the age of maturity." At what age did Jesus begin his ministry? At age 30. It was at this stage of his life that he was at full stature and began His ministry. Before that He was known simply as "the carpenter's son."

In the Old Testament Jewish tradition, the elder women of the young man's household trained his bride. She had left her own family to be his wife. Her husband's extended family had raised him, and they knew his character and personality, so they trained her to be a compatible lifetime partner.

Today in the workplace we're seeing a wide renewal of the mentoring process that has been a part of Jewish culture for thousands of years. Businesses are recognizing the value of pairing employees with those who can offer direction and the knowledge of their experience.

In Western culture we parents do not practice the 17 years of parental management during the age of decision. We emancipate our children at 18 years of age—or they escape on their own. While we have them in the household during their adolescence, we can foster the type of relationship that will bring them to maturity by encouraging them to start making decisions on their own.

When I remarried Judy, our son, Jeff, was 17 years old and a senior in high school. Because of my abuse during our first marriage, I was quite a dictator with Jeff, nearly telling him when he could and could not breathe. I eventually realized that for Jeff's well-being, I had to let him take control of his own life. I told him, "Jeff, I've always run your life, but I'm learning that you need to start making your own decisions while I'm here to be your safety net. I'm not going to set a curfew for you."

I encouraged him, working to establish a relationship through which I would be available for him if he needed mentoring or rescuing. He started making decisions, and his growth accelerated. Twice he made some particularly bad decisions, and Judy and I helped him face the consequences and resolve the conflicts. We wanted to respond to his mistakes with kindness and teaching. He was impressed by how we handled his mistakes, and our relationship grew from that process.

Dependence is primary for a child younger than 13. When the child enters puberty and moves into the age of decision, independence is important. If we make our teenagers deal with their independence without guidance and a helping hand, they will not have guidance as they create their own standards of right and wrong. By looking at the Jewish culture's example, we can see how responsibility is taught to young men and women through example.

The Sin Nature

From a theological standpoint, we must ask how the sin nature impacts this process.

I describe the sin nature as a "virus" introduced into God's perfect computer and software. Because of it, we need a Redeemer. Jer. 17:9 says, "The heart is deceitful above all things, and desperately wicked: who can know it?" (KJV). Our arrested development from the wounds in childhood amplify or magnify our sin nature. The deeper the wounds, the more we act selfishly and childishly. The sin nature complicates matters for those afflicted with arrested development.

For example, our faith walk—even under normal conditions—is tough, because we feel we don't deserve redemption. This leads to a state I call "the foundation of shame." We can't embrace grace and mercy, so we struggle with accepting what's freely given. This is something every person faces, whether he or she has faced childhood trauma or not.

The good news is that despite the fall of humanity and all our personal failings, God has told us that we're the apple of His eye. This gives us all hope.

When we have too much childhood trauma, this hinders our ability to develop genuine healthy relationships with the Creator and others. We can't really reach out or accept others because our wounds have made us unteachable, unable to trust, and afraid of truth.

They Would Not Bow

Prov. 22:6 says, "Train up a child in the way he should go: and when he is old, he will not depart from it" (KJV).

The original Hebrew translation of Prov. 22:6 is more specific on the stages of a child's foundational belief systems. "Train a child in the ways of Jehovah God, or our Creator, and when he grows whiskers he will not depart from the teaching."

Daniel, Shadrach, Meshach, and Abednego were young men when the Babylonians seized Jerusalem. These young men were forced to join an alien, pagan culture after being raised in godly homes and taught to respect Jehovah and the teachings of their elders. All four were singled out as favorites in the king's court because of their strength, wisdom, and judgment. When King Nebuchadnezzar decreed that he alone should be worshiped in Babylonia, Daniel,

Shadrach, Meshach, and Abednego would not bow. The young men were loyal to their God and their training to the point of dying for their belief system.

This happens with children who grow normally, who have not experienced childhood trauma. They grow to be strong and self-confident.

But what of those who have been wounded in their homes? Strangely, we're as loyal to our dysfunctional homes as the Hebrew children were loyal to Jehovah and their godly training. We'll hang on to the pain, willing even to face death rather than to change.

God blessed and delivered Shadrach, Meshach, and Abednego from the fiery furnace they were thrown into after they refused to bow. The lions' mouths were shut when Daniel found himself in their lair after being caught praying to God when he knew it was certain death to do so.

A director in our Life Skills program would once go into a rage at the drop of a word. In three years of teaching the program, she has learned to react differently by delaying her responses and her reactive behavior and by thinking through her feelings and words. Her life has completely changed as a result, and in a sense she illustrates the one who was trained right in childhood and returned to that training after many years. Her life has stabilized. She helps her family members work through their own rage and reactions and has found real peace. She calls it "the joy of growing up."

Any one of us can become like those men and that director: mature, loyal, committed to the truth and to God. To get there, we must take steps to stop our arrested development and move on into full maturity. If we're willing to let him, God can tear down our walls of wounds and help us change.

THIS WAS ^4^ MY CHILDHOOD

My grandson Ben is a genius.

I realize all grandparents feel that way about each of their grandchildren, but I'm confident in Ben's case it's really true. At four years old, Ben could say *entomologist,* and he knew he wanted to be one. He loves bugs.

His grandmother and I live in the country, which is the perfect environment for bug capturing. From our garage to our mudroom are exactly 17 steps made of cement block caps. When Ben comes to our house, he turns each of the 17 steps upside down to discover the dark insect world underneath. This bit of archaeological work rewards him with boxes of bugs to study.

We don't mind Ben's bug boxes, but our backyard resembles a construction zone when he's finished exploring. Of course, I'm responsible to properly replace all the steps. At one point when this got tiring, I gave him new instructions: "Ben, I don't want you to turn over another one of those steps to pick up bugs."

Within five minutes of my issuing this rule, I heard the clinking of the cement steps. I entered the backyard to lovingly discipline the child who had clearly disobeyed my directions.

"Papa! Papa!" Ben cried, aware that punishment was on the way, "You can't punish me, because I never turned a step over. The middle one I lifted up. That one over there I picked up and sat down there. This one here I pulled over to the side." Ben pointed wildly at different steps. "But, Papa, I didn't disobey. I never turned one over!"

Ben's behavior is not bad or shocking. He was a four-year-old. In his child's mind, he believed he wasn't breaking my rule. He just resourcefully found a way around it. Thus, my responsibility as the adult was to explain to Ben exactly what I wanted or didn't want to see happen in my backyard. I didn't do that precisely enough, and Ben took advantage of it. In time, he will learn the broadness of a directive, which may include every scenario.

What happens when we see the same behavior in an adult? An adult should know the difference between turning over the step and lifting the step. A mature adult does not seek loopholes in the system of rights and wrongs. Certainly, on occasion we all try to bend rules to suit our purpose. When justification becomes a pattern or typical behavior, it indicates a lack of maturity and possibly a delay in normal development.

For example, the United States was governed for eight years by a president who swore on television that he did not have a sexual relationship with "that woman," yet we know the rest of the story.

God gave the Ten Commandments so the simplicity of His laws would be enough to set a standard for the nation of Israel. The Pharisees established over 3,000 rules to supplement God's commandments. If we're mature, the seventh commandment, "Thou shalt not commit adultery" (Exod. 20:14, KJV), covers all things in between: too-close friendships with members of the opposite sex to the many sexual perversions common in today's world.

People today tend to search for loopholes in legal matters. In our organization, our contract for services has grown over the past 20 years from an $8^{1}/_{2}$ x 11, double-spaced, single page to four legal-sized pages of small type, single-spaced, because we had no choice but to itemize each detail. People will justify the need to do what they've been told not to do so they can get what they want.

Justification is just one example of an action that's typical for a growing child but not normal for an adult. Early childish behavior in an adult indicates that part of our fundamental maturing process is frozen and that we still need to deal with the issues of our childhood.

By noticing how a child grows, we can examine the stages of his or her life and know what to expect. We may also be able to draw parallels to certain behavior that seems out of place in adults.

What Is Normal Development in a Child?

"Normal" is a term we must use loosely. However, by looking at Erik Erikson's Life Span Chart [*Figure 4-A*], we can see what's typical in the childhood development process. This should challenge you to chart whether or not you had a normal childhood, or it should help you determine if some wounds in childhood have pushed you toward an abnormal, reactive lifestyle.

Birth Bonding

Birth is a radical experience for an infant. After several confusing moments, the baby's entire world changes. No longer surrounded by fluid, being physically connected to a sustaining life source, and feeling the security of the womb, an infant is introduced to a world significantly colder and entirely foreign.

During the baby's time in the womb, he or she has become accustomed to the mother's heartbeat. The child is familiar with the sound of his or her mother's voice, breathing, and the warmth of her body temperature. Mother is the child's safe world.

Within the first hour after delivery, the mother has the chance to re-establish a sense of security for her child. She talks to her baby—that voice is familiar, of course. As she holds the baby tightly, the baby begins to recognize the new place as safe.

A mother will scrutinize her child from head to foot, examining all the fingers and toes. Her touch releases a chemical called cortisol. It is important because it starts the development of motor skills and emotional development. Thus, touch is extremely important.

FIGURE 4-A

ERIK ERICKSON'S SIX LIFE STAGES*

Stage	Age (Approx.)	Task	Aspects of Tasks	If Not Accomplished	Lasting Accomplishment of Successful Outcome
I	Infancy (birth to 1 yr.)	*Basic trust*	Physical and emotional "mothering." A sense of order and stability in the events he or she experiences; feelings of being wanted, loved, and cared for.	*Basic Mistrust.* Life remains chaotic, unconnected. Child is sickly, physically and psychologically disabled. High infant mortality; childhood autism; academic retardation.	*Drive and Hope*
II	Toddler Age (1 to 3 yr.)	*Autonomy*	Learns to stand on own two feet; feeds self, and so on. Controls bodily functions. Makes basic needs known through language. Discovers choices; learns to say "no" and "yes." Accepts "no" as well as "yes." Learns the rules of society; "may and may not do."	*Shame and Doubt.* Lack of autonomy produces passive dependence on others; unable to assert own will results in overobedience; unable to accept "no" results in personality constantly rebellious; perhaps "delinquent."	*Self-Control and Will Power*
III	Preschool Age (about 4 to 6 yr.)	*Initiative*	Learns geography and time, can go and come back, can think in terms of future, has developed memory, learns beginning adult roles. More loving, cooperative, secure in family. Good chance of becoming a "moral" person.	*Guilt.* Wants always to be in control. Sense of competition drives person to be "overcompetitive"; may be always outside law.	*Direction and Purpose*
IV	School Age (about 6 to 12 yr.)	*Industry*	Learning the "how tos" of society; in Western society masters "3 Rs"; begins to understand matrices of society. Learns to feel worthy and competent.	*Inferiority.* If person fails to learn industry, begins to feel inferior compared to others. If overlearns industry, may become too "task oriented" and overconforms to society.	*Method and Competence*
V	Adolescence (12 to late teens or early adulthood)	*Identity*	Sexual maturation and sexual identity. Discovers role in life; ponders question "Who am I?" as distinct from family. Develops social friendships; rejects family.	*Role Confusion.* May not achieve a personal identity separate from family. May not become socially adult or sexually stable.	*Devotion and Fidelity*
VI	Early Adulthood	*Intimacy*	Learns to share passions, interests, problems with another individual. Learns to think of "we," "our," "us" instead of "I," "my," or "me." Affiliates with others; family, place of work, community. Achieves stability.	*Isolation.* Inability to be intimate with others. Becomes fixated at adolescent level of sensation seeking and self-pleasure. Avoids responsibility. Lacks "roots" and stability.	*Affiliation and Love*

*The first six stages of Erickson's eight stages are dealt with here.
Adapted from Erik H. Erickson, *Identity and the Life Cycle* (New York and London: W. W. Norton and Co., 1980).

As we experience birth bonding with our mother, our software confirms that being born is safe and good. We need to know that this is our mother and that we're in a safe place. This first experience, along with the continued nurture we receive in childhood, lays the foundation for normal development.

Normal Early Childhood

As we grow, we constantly learn and develop new skills and abilities. Let's look at several normal developmental stages for children.

The child doesn't know where he or she ends and Mommy begins. The child in the womb and his or her mother are one. The whole life of a child up to the time of birth naturally involves being connected to Mommy. But after birth, that bonding doesn't change for several months. It's normal that the child is enmeshed with his or her mother and totally dependent on her.

As the child grows into the crawling stage, Mommy becomes a base from which to explore securely. The baby crawls away a few feet and looks back quickly to make sure Mommy is still there. In the first year, Mommy will try many times to help her child complete a task, and the child will try to do it on his or her own and fail. As a result, the child sees that Mommy will fix whatever goes wrong in his or her world. At this age, the child also learns that if people respond to him or her, he or she must have value. This is normal and leads to the need to be the center of attention.

The child doesn't know where he or she ends and the world begins. This is a second primary stage in the child's life. Here he or she develops a conscience. Mommy's conscience is the foundation of the conscience. What Mommy likes and talks about is what the child likes and talks about. From 15 months to 2½ years is critical in the development of a child's conscience. He or she learns obedience by the directives and boundaries his or her parents establish and learns consequences through praise or discipline from the parents.

What is the necessary ingredient for establishing a sol-

id, God-honoring conscience? Consistency. Without consequences for unacceptable behavior and praise for acceptable behavior, a child does not develop a conscience. As a
result, he or she will be manipulative and controlling for a
lifetime. This is the stage we call the terrible two's—in
which children constantly test their world. They will try to
become their own authority, the center of their universe,
and they believe the world revolves around their desires.
This is normal and important for their learning as they discover the importance of boundaries and consequences. To
the child's software, boundaries, directives, and consequences prove they are loved. Proper discipline equals validation, attention, and love.

Seeing themselves as the center of the universe, children believe all they see belongs to them. They cannot delay their responses or control impulses. Young children are
totally reactive to their world.

"If I can't see it, it doesn't exist." In a recent McDonald's
commercial, a baby swings in front of a window. When the
swing is high, he can see the McDonald's arches and
smiles. When the swing is low, he can no longer see the
arches and cries.

Seeing his or her mother walk out the door, the child
doesn't realize Mommy still exists beyond what he or she
can see. Also at this stage, the child believes he or she must
possess whatever he or she is focused upon: Mommy, a toy,
a friend, and so on. For a youngster, possession leads to the
need to control and to the fear of loss. The youngster does
not know how to let go of what is seen as his or her possession, and he or she will do anything to find what's been
lost. He or she will focus solely on that object or person until it's under his or her control again.

We will disrupt the world to get our way. A child at this
level will disrupt the world to get what he or she wants. I
was in a meeting with several adults and a well-known
speaker. A three-year-old girl in the meeting with her parents began to throw a tantrum. The speaker soon asked the
parents to take their child out of the meeting. This little girl
didn't comprehend that others were in the room, or the im-

portance of the speaker. She was completely focused on her wants and how to get them regardless of those around her.

This is commonly called a temper tantrum. A child will see his or her disruption as a successful effort to get everyone's attention. This is not unusual or bad—it just symbolizes our desire to have our wants and needs met first and foremost.

The following list shows how a child thinks and the reason directives and discipline are critical.

- The child has no understanding or recognition of those in authority.
- The child has no understanding of consideration or respect for others.
- The child cannot control impulses.
- The child's wants, not needs, dominate.
- The child's wants and ability to get those wants will override the consequences.
- The child wants immediate gratification and doesn't understand waiting.
- The child lives now. Tomorrow doesn't exist.

Parallel play. In this stage, the child typically sits close to others but plays with separate games or toys. A child at this stage does not understand that he or she is part of a family or community, instead seeing himself or herself as the center of his or her world. The child's mind-set is "Stay out of my world unless I let you in." "I'm unable to share." "Don't touch my stuff." "What's mine is mine, and what's yours is mine, too."

Begrudging sharing. This phase soon moves into a later stage of development in which the child begins to share only when forced to.

Imagine two little boys, Joey and Corbin, sitting on a blanket at a picnic. Both are playing together separately with their toys. Joey suddenly reaches over and grabs Corbin's truck. Corbin quickly reacts and snatches the toy back, smacking Joey on the head with the truck. Corbin's mother sees the incident and takes the truck from Corbin, giving it back to Joey. She scolds Corbin for his unwillingness to share.

Is this unusual? No, Corbin is a normal child. From this

experience, his reactions are (1) a lack of respect for the authority, Mommy, who gave his truck away; (2) a fear that he has lost his truck forever; (3) a resolve that he'll be more protective in controlling the rest of his toys; (4) an increase in his desire for *that* truck; and (5) trusting only himself, projecting his anger on anyone who will listen.

Compartmental thinking. This element appears in a child's inability to see things in perspective. The child cannot see a situation from the beginning to end. As we mentioned earlier, children before puberty cannot think in hypothetical or abstract terms. They also cannot make the connection between boundaries and consequences. They learn this connection through experience, discipline, and consistency. A child in this stage and age has an all-or-nothing thinking process—with no middle ground or balance. This makes the child very rigid in his or her thinking and behavior. At this stage, a child thinks in fragments and cannot piece together the entire picture.

Authority and the Healthy Child

To a healthy child, authority equals provision, protection, leadership, training, promise, security, commitment, safety, love, and conflict resolution. When a father disciplines his child, we can all hear in our minds the child asking, "Do you still love me, Daddy?" The question surfaces after Daddy's new flashlight has been broken or a cup of chocolate ice cream has redecorated the back seat of his car. Unable to recognize that Daddy's love is unconditional, a child fears his or her mistake will cause the loved one to stop loving him or her. With consistent love, direction, and nurture, the child will learn that love is safe and does not depend on what is done, but who he or she is.

The Wounded Child

Although the behavior described above is not always desirable in a child and needs correction, it's still normal. But what happens in the wounded child?

If the child exhibits the following symptoms, he or she may be experiencing a wound of some kind.

Ease of being intimidated. After an initial wound, some children are easily bullied and continually intimidated.

Isolation and mood swings. Wounded children may withdraw and be moody, afraid that each person will be angry or upset with them.

Withdrawn anger and "Why me?" Children may become angry with themselves because they believe they have caused the abuse.

Escalating rebellion. A wounded child loses his or her self-esteem and finds it hard to believe that Mommy and Daddy could love him or her if they knew the truth. The child continually tests his or her parents by rebelling. The parents can never love enough; the child can never receive enough love.

Restlessness. The body responds to the child's feelings of defectiveness by producing adrenaline for survival. The chemical was given to us by our Creator for fight-or-flight situations

Nightmares. Our minds want to resolve our conflicts, but if the conflicts are left unresolved, our minds will repeat our problems over and over in the form of disturbing dreams.

Inattentiveness (ADD/ADHD). After I was abused in third grade, my schoolwork dropped from excellent to my nearly failing. Today, I would have been diagnosed with ADD/ADHD (attention deficit disorder/attention deficit hyperactivity disorder) and would be prescribed Ritalin. In school, each grade becomes more intense, because educators assume the child is developing naturally. A wounded child is less successful because he or she cannot progress.

Preoccupation and daydreaming. These two mind-sets are early escape methods designed to release us from the pain we feel from our wounds.

Hostility and aggression. In our struggle to control our world, we can exhibit this in many ways, especially in physical violence, like kicking and biting, abusing pets, starting fires, or bullying younger children.

Not only does the wounded child exhibit the preceding behaviors all the time, but he or she will also deny these be-

haviors to himself or herself and others in the following
ways:

- *Blame shifting.* The child refuses to accept accountability for his or her disobedience, pointing the finger
  at others. "Johnny did it!" or "It wasn't me!"
- *Minimizing.* Never wanting to own mistakes, the child
  will downplay the circumstances or situation.
- *Denial.* Outright lying about the situation or circum-
  stance.
- *Poor memory.* When questioned, answers by saying, "I
  don't know" or "I don't remember."

Security

The wounded child's sense of security has been severely
compromised, resulting in a sense of powerlessness. Those
of us who were wounded as children were not able to control what happened in our lives. Our parents weren't able
to protect us. Many times our parents didn't even know we
were wounded. The emotions tied with the incident are
seared into the circuit board of our brain. Wounds that
we've forgotten for the sake of self-preservation begin to
drive our behaviors.

Children are powerless, but as they grow, they begin to
take steps of independence. These wounds and symptoms
add up to a dangerous perception of powerlessness, which
sets the stage for rage and creates an impulse for revenge
that carries into adulthood. These children grow into
teenagers, dealing with the onset of new hormones and all
the complicated emotions involved with this new stage in
life, already wounded.

I believe this is an element involved in school shootings. Through our program, we have worked with teenagers
from Columbine High School of Littleton, Colorado. The
teens who were not shot but are traumatized seem mostly
to be those who have never experienced close relationships
with their parents. They feel alone. They feel rage and suffer from low self-esteem. Though the shooting was several
years ago, the students still hurt and feel powerless. Many
don't want to go to school. But those who have bonded with

and sense the love and commitment of their parents have come through the trauma. Those who did not have that experience still struggle.

We're trying to restore the maturing process. A group of children from various schools where shootings have occurred recently attended a conference in California, and one of our directors saw tremendous progress through these teens' sharing and connecting with the maturing process.

How is that accomplished? We'll look at that problem in the chapters ahead.

5

THE HURTING CHILD BECOMES THE TROUBLED TEEN

In one of comedian Jim Carrey's early films, *The Mask*, he played the role of Stanley Ipkiss, a quiet and lonely bank clerk. Stanley's world changes radically when his dog drags home an ancient artifact—a mask. When slipped onto Stanley's head, it transforms him into a vivacious, green character with a mad desire for dancing, damsels in distress, and saving the day. Once altered by the mask, Carrey's character makes bold moves that his mild-mannered banking self would never be brave enough to try.

Wide audiences were drawn to *The Mask* for several reasons besides the obvious one—Carrey's comedic talents. The idea of being someone else appeals to many of us. Being able to hide our true identity creates a sense of security—we seem to think we can't be hurt if our inner person remains hidden.

As a wounded child grows into the teen years, he or she has an especially difficult time finding identity and maturing well.

I've enjoyed *Children Are Wet Cement,* by Anne Ortlund, which tells about how children process. The "cement" of the brain hardens when the chemicals of puberty begin to be released, usually when a child reaches eight to nine years of age. The new chemical structure in the adolescent brain helps the teen start thinking in logical, rational, abstract, and hypothetical realms. At this point, our wounds solidify. We now believe the lie and our distorted perception of ourselves.

All teenagers struggle with identity. They're rarely comfortable with their physical and emotional selves during these difficult years. Healthy teenagers may act differently around parents and peers, but they're fundamentally the same persons with either group. A growing teen may take a personal phone call behind locked doors, laugh at different jokes than they would at your dinner table, or not want to be seen with you at the mall. Typical teenage behavior dictates a fair amount of stretching space and room for personality quirks, but a mask that is worn consistently at home is different. This indicates two separate personalities.

Wounded children growing into teenagers quickly discover the benefit of developing a chameleon-like face for the worlds in which they live. After all, acceptance as teens is difficult enough without revealing that they're hurting inside. They discover they have good reason to bury their anger and feelings when authority figures, adults, peers, and family members all expect certain behaviors.

Because of our wounds, the undeveloped core character drives our behavior. We become reactive, and the anger under the surface builds and contaminates our behavior. We become who we want to be depending on how it suits our needs. A hurting adolescent moves from a childish personality based on emotional survival to manipulating to seek validation. We're always motivated to control people, situations, and circumstances to our advantage.

My potential to develop two distinct personalities was not the life God intended for me. As James 1:8 says, "A double minded man is unstable in all his ways" (KJV). As an angry teen in junior high school, I had already established an unhealthy personality. At home or in church, I was the model Christian young man, doing and saying the right things. Outside the home and away from church, I wore a different face. I acted out my rage through dirty stories, cursing, and violence.

Teens recognize the duality of their peers, and as I stated earlier in this book, the kids of our church took stories home to their families, and eventually parents of my friends confronted my mother about my erratic behavior. My mask was so firmly established that my mother trustingly alienated her friends and fellow parishioners to defend me. She also didn't want to face the possibility that I could truly be that type of person.

The parents of Dylan Klebold and Eric Harris, the two young men who opened fire in Columbine High School on April 20, 1999, claimed they never saw any signs of this danger in their children. Yet these young men were building bombs in their very homes.

Shifts in the Mask

The wounded teen reacts outside the home and conforms inside the home. After marriage, the wounded adult will react *in* the home and conform *outside* the home. The pressures of conforming both in the home with a new spouse and outside the home are too great for the wounded adult. Within six to seven months of being married, often the worst behavior surfaces in the home, and the shift begins. A person arrested in development will use the duality to manipulate and has total control of which personality he or she uses.

SIGNS OF A WOUNDED TEEN

Refinement of Self-Doubt

By the time the child is a teenager, he or she has fine-tuned his or her self-doubt to be used and controlled on impulse. That person may live with self-doubt for the rest of his or her life until he or she learns how to move beyond the childhood wounds.

The wounds of childhood, along with the feeling of being defective, will cause wounded teens to gravitate toward other wounded teens. Gang life is tied to this search for peers with similar identity. Wounded teens lacking father figures and validation find security in this violent, dysfunctional "family." They want to feel a part of a comfortable community in which they can express their pain and be accepted. In sharing their wounds, they don't feel isolated.

Cliques in schools are not very different from gangs. All kids want is to be a part of something that validates them where they are. The search for acceptance is a natural drive of puberty.

Manipulation and Control

Because of the wounds of childhood, our decisions are often made by circumstances and other people. This leaves us feeling powerless. In the teen years, we compensate for this perception of powerlessness by going to extremes to control every area of our lives. We're so out of control that we must try to control everything else in some way. We must realize that we have no power to control anyone or anything except ourselves.

Fulfillment of Rejection

The Bible tells us that we're to love our neighbor as ourselves. When we've been wounded, we feel flawed and rejected and lose our self-esteem. If we can't find our value, we'll never find value in anyone else. We can't give away what we don't possess. Expecting to be rejected becomes our way of life.

Sabotage

A wounded person might sabotage anything good that comes into his or her life because that person may think he or she is not worthy of anything good happening. The wounded person thinks, *If people knew how defective I really am, they would reject me, and I would lose the good things in my life. Better for me to sabotage my blessings than to receive them and have them taken away by someone else.*

Many teenagers have had the opportunity to develop a balanced relationship with a healthy partner and have chosen to sabotage that relationship. They thought it would be better never to experience the joy of unconditional love than to have it and then lose it. With our attitudes and behavior, we drive that wonderful person out of our lives. We live in self-pity, crying, "Why me?" "God knows I tried!" and "If only things were different!"

Selfishness and Self-Centeredness

Teenagers who are very self-centered don't truly feel worthy of any positive experience that comes along. No one can get through the mask. Children who have been wounded will often feel selfishness and unworthy feelings in their teen years. These wounds disable their ability to become part of something greater. Wounded teens build walls to hide behind and cannot function in a team environment. Many times they can't work in a structured job because of the time clock and the boss's authority. They may also find it hard to deal with marriage, seeing their partner as an authority figure and not as part of a team. They even struggle with the authority of God and the structure of a faith system.

Promiscuity

As sexual opportunities increase, wounded teens who feel rejected often seek validation through their sexuality. When a child is abused sexually, the perpetrator has established the child's worth as a sexual object. The child will now believe his or her value is sexual. Sexual abuse is directly tied to the pain of rejection.

Being promiscuous may be the only safe way sexually abused teens feel they can connect. Without the emotional bond, however, the physical involvement typically results in shame. In this cycle, teens don't want to get emotionally involved. They are withholding that type of affection, seeing it as true intimacy and saving it for someone they see in their fantasy relationship in the future.

Promiscuity leads to a repeating pattern of sexual activity and isolation. Teenagers are sensitive, but as the cycle continues to repeat itself, they harden their emotions and struggle to bond emotionally to others.

Self-Mutilation

Teens sometimes self-mutilate for several reasons. One possible reason is that by cutting their bodies, they're trying to numb the emotional pain by causing physical pain on which to focus. Physical pain is easier for such teens to accept. They will self-mutilate again and again to keep the pain on a *physical* level.

Eating Disorders

Overeating. When emotional pain becomes unbearable, a teen may overeat as a source of comfort. If sexual abuse has occurred in childhood, obesity may become a protection. The teen believes that if he or she is heavy, is unattractive, and dresses unattractively, his or her appearance will be a protection against any sexual contact. In the search for a lifetime partner, many times the wounded teen looks for someone who will see beyond his or her physical appearance and find the inner value that the teen can't find in himself or herself.

Bulimia/anorexia. These eating disorders may serve as escape mechanisms and rewards. With bulimia we comfort ourselves with food then punish ourselves by purging. Anorexia often is a manifestation in children or teens who base their value on their physical appearance. This fulfills the popular lie "You can never be thin enough."

Isolation

The teen years are about learning we're not alone in this world. We realize we're part of a bigger picture and that others like us are out there. In junior high or high school, teens become involved in drama, band, choir, baseball, soccer, football, basketball, cheerleading, and various other team activities. This encourages them to work in units instead of being "lone rangers." Many times wounded teens don't want to be part of something greater for fear of failure. If the team fails, the wounded teen will take responsibility for the failure. That's not a risk wounded teens want to take.

Flashbacks

By denying our wounds of childhood, we consciously shut the door on painful experiences of the past. A flashback, like a still photograph of the incident, will surprise us like lightning. If by adolescence we've not dealt with these issues that are beginning to warp our reality, the mind will give us glimpses of those "photos"—but not the entire picture. We quickly doubt the authenticity of what we're seeing and repress the memory even further. Many times as we grow older, we'll lose memory of the wound but will continue to react with our unacceptable behaviors.

Blame Shifting

We shift blame of our reactive behaviors to people, situations, and circumstances. We do this for the simple reason of excusing our own behavior.

Justification

When we can't change what we know we should, we will then justify our behaviors and our attitudes in childish ways. Many times we'll use scripture out of context, other people's opinions, and irrational thought processes to justify what we know is not acceptable.

Judgmental and Critical Attitude

Shame is the foundation for self-rejection and the rejection of others. We perceive that we must criticize and judge others to elevate ourselves. This creates intense isolation and builds walls.

Authority

With the onset of puberty, wounded teenagers will begin to experience serious problems with authority. After being wounded and losing their security system, they become their own authority, desperately attempting to create a safe place for themselves. Their safety becomes an illusion.

When classes resumed at Columbine High School in the fall of 1999 following the April shooting, educators and parents noticed that students were leaving their homes in the mornings yet weren't showing up for school.

What was happening?

Every day students walk into their school buildings. The school represents a place of learning, authority, and safety with adults who, in an ideal world, should be able to take care of and protect the students. Authority represents safety, protection, provision, and promise.

But all of that failed at Columbine. One student said, "A favorite teacher died in the tragedy, so the authority of the school couldn't even protect its own, let alone the students. Why would they want to return to the school? Twelve of the students and a teacher died in that school. It did not feel safe regardless of how many times they wanted to rebuild the library."

Teens reason that if their authority—in this case the school and in many cases a parent—won't or can't protect them, they will become their own authority. They feel they have no choice for self-preservation.

On the Inside

Internally, the struggle to mature will leave a wounded adolescent feeling lost, insecure, and unloved. The wounds have left a gaping hole where real needs are not being met.

If the teen has suffered rejection, we must encourage him or her to become the person he or she would like to be. We need to give gentle direction and guidance at this point in the maturation process.

If the teen fell victim to sexual abuse, he or she needs to know it wasn't his or her fault. If the teen experienced physical or mental abuse, he or she will feel powerless, intimidated, and indecisive. These persons need constant validation and encouragement.

How Can I Help My Teen?

- Create a safe place in which the wounded teen can express wounds, emotions, anger, feelings, and fears.
- Validate the teen by expressing the value you see in him or her. Itemize positive qualities and repeat the validation often. As mentioned previously, you can say, "Nothing you can do, nothing you can say, and

nothing you can tell me about yourself will cause me not to love you."

- Confront the behavior. Always remember to separate the wrong behavior from the high value of the teen. Remind wounded teens that their actions must be confronted and consequences must be consistently enforced—but that does not change the fact that you love them.
- Identify the problem with which the teen is struggling. Offer options for the resolution of that problem.

As a parent, it's your duty to mentor that teen, help resolve the conflicts, and help bring change to the behavior.

One example of such a parent is Jill. She told me her son had been very detached through his teen years. They had never bonded. She went to her son and offered to listen to him, to create a safe place where he could share his pain. She said, "He started to talk, and we're working through these conflicts. We've seen tremendous change. He has even taken an interest in spiritual things and wants to go back to church." She had battled for years trying to connect with him, and this small effort did it.

The Wounded Teen Moves On

As the teen prepares to leave the adolescent years, the journey to single adulthood is devastating if the inner conflicts remain unresolved. He or she is leaving the supervised family and escaping consequences yet is unable to make decisions that are not driven by pain.

What will happen in adulthood? We'll look at that next.

6
I'M SINGLE, ON MY OWN— IS THIS ALL THERE IS?

Many teens see the completion of high school as a jumping-off point. They feel they face countless options: college, career, travel, and romance. They think their lives can finally begin. "I'm in charge now and don't have to follow the rules, supervision, and discipline of my parents. I can now be who I want to be." The sky's the limit!

In our culture, the teenager leaves home for a life outside the boundaries of the controlled environment of the family. For the average young person, this is probably not a difficult transition. But the wounded teen generally hasn't been prepared yet for the age of maturity, or full stature. Training for a lifetime of important decisions should have begun in the home with people who care and will support the teen as he or she grows. But for the wounded person, this did not happen.

Out of Bounds

The wounded teenager leaving home is desperate for new freedom. This is compounded by the powerlessness he or she has felt for years. Without the authority he or she has so long resisted, the teenager pushes new limits.

The greater problem is that the earlier the wounds were inflicted, the more people need rules. They need rules to release them of the responsibility of their behavior. They

make the rules they depend on responsible for their salvation, yet they fight against personal accountability and
commitment. The nation of Israel added rules to structure
their society and to supplement the concise Ten Commandments God gave Moses on Mt. Sinai. Nearly every element
of their culture was structured by regulations they created.
They recognized their inability to create their own boundaries and to live by them.

In my seminars I use the example of the teenager whose
parents set a firm curfew and forbade him to drink alcohol
while living in their house. The young man turned 18,
moved into a studio apartment as soon as possible, and
bought a case of beer his first night out on his own. He
stayed up all night sitting alone in his truck and drank the
entire case of beer. This young man defied his parents for
one simple reason: now he could. The rules were ended.
Time to party!

When we're wounded, we have a childish perception
and will fight rules because they represent the authority
that failed us when we were young. We need the rules to
structure our lives, but we battle them intensely. We justify
our reasons and say we can't live out the rules, but we fail
to see the consequences of breaking them.

What We Need

Out of the family household and on our own, we're free
to pursue our dreams and desires to the fullest extent. If
we're healthy in mind, body, and spirit, young adulthood is
the point at which we can start building a future. Most ex-
plorations of self begin with fulfilling basic needs—shelter,
food, education—and then moving on from there.

A recent film featured the story of a man who was able
to hear women's thoughts. His psychologist told him he
had received a great gift—the ability to know what women
want and need. Because he could hear their thoughts, he
could meet their needs, and his female friends therefore
adored him.

Likewise, if we cannot identify our needs, we'll probably
never get them met. God knows our needs before we ask.

Babies demonstrate their neediness through fussiness, crying, or throwing temper tantrums, but they can't say, "I need to be fed. I need a hug. I need to sleep."

If we're still harboring wounds, though, we'll be unable to communicate what we need. Both women and men tend to expect their partner or the person they love to possess that nonexistent gift of knowing their needs and meeting them. The rationale is that "If they really loved me, they would know what I need and would meet those needs." This is a losing scenario. Yet this is the way the wounded individual thinks, even if the person isn't sure what his or her needs are.

The Fantasy and the Reality

Our struggle translates into even further problems when we look for that special person to develop a relationship with, as happens during this stage of life. Our minds develop a fantasy person to meet those needs we can't even pinpoint. This sets us up for failure, for many issues that wounded husbands and wives deal with in their marriage are carried over from their wounds of childhood.

We wounded people should have resolved these issues before we dated anyone, let alone married. We then spend the rest of our lives trying to make our partner resolve our pre-existing conflicts. When we resolve our childhood issues, we then have a foundation to find marriage counseling to be rewarding. Without resolving pre-existing conflicts, the healthy adult-to-adult relationship will end up emulating a child-parent relationship. This is totally foreign to the software the Creator instilled in us to help us experience the joy of a marital relationship.

When we recognize that we have many conflicts caused by our childhood wounds, we need to seek professional counseling or help to resolve the conflicts and salvage our relationship. Issues this complex cannot be solved in the home, as wounded husbands and wives generally won't receive counseling from each other. This is complicated by the fact that the deeper our wounds are, the higher our expectations will be toward our partners. On a scale of 1 to 10,

UNHEALTHY EXPECTATIONS RANGE	10 9 8 7 6 5 4 3 2	My expectations of others demands a performance at a 9 level in order for me to accept it and be satisfied by it. If my expectations are not met, I become critical and judgmental to establish justification for my feelings of superiority over them, and I rationalize my anger.
HEALTHY EXPECTATIONS RANGE	1 Normal 1	The more I heal and move up the chart toward normal, the more my expectations of others moves down the chart into a more normal area. Now when my realistic expectations are not met, I am still intact. I have not been rejected. I realize that I have value in spite of deep trauma in my life.
DEPTH OF TRAUMA	2 3 4 5 6 7 8 9 10	If I have been wounded at the 9 level depth of trauma, then I feel worthless, and my development is arrested.

if I were wounded at a level of 9 (a very deep wound), I would expect my partner to be above normal to the point that I would expect a 9 on the upper end of the scale (see chart below) to overcompensate for the depth of my wound. Thus, I set an unrealistic, impossible, unattainable expectation that turns into inner rage. Many times this causes me to explode and withdraw from others.

When we're wounded as children, we drag our unresolved conflicts and reactive behaviors from childhood into adolescence. We then drag our teenage frustrations into single adulthood. We eventually enter a commitment or marriage with a sack full of attitudes, emotions, and reactive behaviors attached to our backs. We can't tear it off. The bigger the crisis we face in our relationship, the more we will regress to childishness in our reactions.

Reactive Behaviors in Single Adulthood

What happens under these conditions? Consider some of the following:

We erect barriers. We need to be alone and in control of our life, but we cannot do either. We have escaped the authority we have resented. Our loss of self-esteem, though, has led us to erect huge barriers, which is ultimately a survival technique we developed in childhood.

Self-doubt is now in place. Esteem is now unattainable. We focus on the past. We always look back. Nothing in the future looks promising, and we have no hope of change. Instead of looking toward relationships and success, we become workaholics. We seek validation through our performances.

Rebellion is refined. If we hate ourselves, then we hate others. We become judgmental. We live in self-pity. We live in massive confusion. We become confused about our identity, our goals, our needs, and our desires. Unable to make decisions, we lose our stability and fear tomorrow. We then look for someone to take care of us, because we feel like children in a world of adults. We feel like the eternal victims.

We keep a "safe" distance from spirituality: Judgmental, critical, and lacking any ability to trust others, we struggle in finding relationships with others—especially our Creator. We're angry with God and want to blame Him for our perceived defectiveness.

We must learn to deal with love and authority in our spiritual lives. Nonetheless, we fight accepting love and authority. As a result, we see God as a hammer, a tyrant who wants only to punish us. The blessing of authority is that it offers protection and provision—especially in a healthy home. If we're whole, that truth is even more evident. But when we're wounded in our childhood, we have no ability to see authority as protective. We can't find God, because we have become our own authorities. We have become our own authority because we doubt truth and fear knowledge. In this stage, we make up our own truth and live our own lies, and we fear God's truth will expose us.

We assert our independence. Looking back at the young man staying up alone and drinking, we can see an example of our desperate need for independence. We want to be independent in our activities, but emotionally we seek someone to become dependent upon. We need to release the emotional pain we're carrying and start the maturing process of taking control of our own lives.

We accelerate promiscuity and sexual problems. We increase our sexual activity because we don't know how to relate in other ways. We want to connect on a relational level, but we don't really know how to have a meaningful, emotionally stable relationship.

We play games. Because of our arrested development, our lives are extremely unstable. We start projects we can't finish, we make promises we can't fulfill, we dream dreams that are impossible, and we struggle with day-to-day survival. In self-pity, we play these games:

"If only . . ." I had a better childhood, more money, a happier marriage . . .

"Woe is me . . ." I'm always the victim. It always happens to me. Nothing ever goes right.

"God knows I've tried . . . " to be a better person, make people happy, achieve my dreams.

"Why me?"

Because actions speak louder than words, we have no creditability with those around us—especially our husband or wife.

The Finish Line

With each of the various women in my life, I never knew what I needed. I drained the energy out of each relationship because I could not pinpoint my needs. I just knew I wasn't getting what I needed, and I reacted like a child. No one in my life could feel she could reach the finish line with me, because I continually moved and changed the boundaries (finish lines). God showed me that I had to identify my needs so that the people in my life could have a "finish line."

What is a finish line? It is clearly defining a need, and then identifying whether that need can be met by ourselves, our partners, or jointly. By establishing a finish line, we can face the need as a couple. When we recognize our needs, we can also bring them to God, and He will be able to meet them. Finally, in light of all He has done, we can bring our worship and praise to Him freely and gladly. Determining a finishing line for our needs is crucial, because it will radically change our relationships with both our loved ones and our Creator.

Steps to a Healthy Relationship

God has instilled within our software the processes needed to build the foundation of a healthy and rewarding relationship. A relationship such as this will continue to grow for a lifetime.

The Word of God offers our blueprint for this. This software mandates that we abstain from sexual activity until a commitment of marriage is in place. We then go through the process of building a relationship and making a commitment in this order:

1. **Gift of attraction**
   - Attraction is what brings the couple together at first. The man looks at the outside, or the physical, and decides what is attractive to him.
   - The woman looks at what's going on internally and

emotionally. Can he communicate? Is he gentle? Does he express his emotions, his fears, his goals, and his dreams? Can he deal with his anger? Does he have character?

2. **Friendship (four levels)**

   Acquaintance
   - Be alert to each new person around you
   - Have a cheerful, friendly countenance; smile
   - Learn and remember the person's name
   - Greet the person by name
   - Ask him or her appropriate questions that reflect interest and acceptance
   - Be a good listener

   Casual friendship (based on common interests)
   - Discover the other person's strong points
   - Learn about his or her hopes and desires
   - Develop and ask appropriate specific questions
   - Show interest and concern if the person shares problems with you
   - Be honest about yourself
   - Reflect interest and trustworthiness in being a friend

   Close Friendship (Based on common interest in the person's future)
   - See potential achievement in the other person's life
   - Discover and discuss that person's specific goals
   - Assume an interest in the development of the person's goals
   - Discern the conflicts that hinder the development of these goals
   - Be creative in encouraging the person to design projects that would help him or her develop and achieve these goals
   - Learn how to encourage the person to build interest for those projects

   Intimate friendship (Based on common interest and commitment to develop each other's character)
   - Learn how to comfort the other through trials and sorrows

- Assume personal interest in the person's reputation
- Be sensitive to traits and attitudes that need to be improved in yourself and in that person
- Discern basic causes of character deficiencies
- Build interest in and awareness of these deficiencies; ask the person to tell you about your faults
- Be committed to faithfulness, loyalty, and availability while setting boundaries and guidelines.

Our relationships should develop from very close friendships.

3. Relationship (four stages)

- **Me to Me**. *Time to evaluate what I bring to the relationship.* When Judy and I started seeing each other the second time around, we spent many months developing the four levels of friendship. I had never even achieved the first level of friendship in our first marriage, yet we had produced three children and were married nearly 17 years. As we developed the four levels of friendship the second time around, I started to see Judy's value in a way I had never seen it before. I began to wonder if potential existed to reconcile our marriage. I used what I call the "me-to-me" relationship. I realized that I wanted to pursue the relationship with Judy, so I itemized on paper the things I could bring to the relationship. I also itemized areas I needed to work on in my desire to find healing. Being brutally honest with myself, I met with Judy again, and we discussed the potential of reconciliation. I shared with her the things I was learning and trying to change about myself. The other list was of items I began working on that may actually take a lifetime to achieve. Through this, we built our second relationship on honesty.
- **Multiple-A**. *Going out with a group but not as a couple.* Because of the trust that had been broken in our first marriage, Judy was still afraid of being alone with me. We decided to attend church together and

go together to some of our son Jeff's concerts at high school. We drove in separate cars and met in the group dynamic. We were together, but with no dating commitment. This let her see me as I socialized, met people, and was comfortable in the group. It built trust.

- **Multiple-B.** *Going out with a group as a couple.* Judy and I then started to go out in groups as a couple. She was starting to trust me enough to let me pick her up at her home, and we could go together. The fear was gone. (I realize we are talking about our personal recovery, but we have found this pattern to be very effective for singles who are starting to date, because each one can see how the other operates in a social setting without the pressure of a dating commitment). We then moved to exclusive dating.

- **Exclusive.** *Dating no others. Finding common values.* At this stage we started to build a relationship, find common values, and validate each other.

4. Going steady, or the promise time

This time helps a couple define what love really is and look at the question "Do I want to invest myself in this person?"

5. Engagement period.

Engagement is a time to focus on emotional bonding, communicating dreams and goals, expressing views and opinions, and sharing perceptions. This is also a time of disclosure. We can share our traumas and wounds of childhood and how we've responded to those wounds. This is where we decide if we need counseling to resolve issues before we marry. The third goal of the engagement period is to look at the history of each family. What, in both families, should we bring into the relationship, and what do we want to leave out of our relationship from our families of origin?

6. Commitment of marriage.

If a young person follows this pattern, each person's value has been established. Both people know they are loved for who they are, and they can realistically become two individuals who choose to develop a new partnership called "we." They choose to form a healthy lifetime commitment—allowing the individuality, personality, and character of each to remain intact.

If the steps are followed, this will lead to a beautiful sexual intimacy that will last a lifetime. When we bypass these steps by going directly from attraction to sexual intimacy, it creates a sexual bonding that causes addictive behavior and a dependent/codependent relationship.

The person who has been wounded in his or her childhood doesn't have the patience or strength of character to go through the steps to a healthy relationship. Like a child, he or she is more interested in instant gratification.

Our unrecognized wounds and unidentified needs also often cause us to become attracted to the wrong people. We search for our fantasy, for the one person who will make everything better for us. Ultimately, this results in disastrous, dysfunctional relationships.

One young woman came to our program after three abusive relationships. The guys she dated pressured her for sex, and she wanted to remain pure. Her last relationship involved a young man who became a stalker. This man threatened her by methods like cutting her tires and pouring acid onto her vehicle.

She came to the seminar asking, "Why do I keep getting into these relationships?"

She discovered her worth in Christ and the power to make choices. She realized she was worth receiving love from someone who was balanced and could treat her properly. She has now moved on to build good and positive relationships. She has found the joy of being whole and is selective in whom she dates.

How can we heal ourselves as this young woman did and move into true adulthood and normalcy?

We'll look at that next.

WHY AM I ⁷ ATTRACTED TO THE WRONG PEOPLE?

Several years ago when I was conducting a workshop in Minneapolis, a woman attended who had been very vocal in her pastor's dismissal from her church. In front of our entire group and her former pastor, the woman stood and explained in detail how he did not meet her needs. The pastor sat quietly in the back, his head in his hands.

"What did you need from him?" I asked. She was silent.

I called her by name and again asked her what she needed from him. More silence. After I asked a third time, she began to sob.

"I don't know," she finally answered.

"If *you* don't know what *you* need," I questioned, "how can *he* know what you need? If you can't identify your needs, don't expect them to be fulfilled."

I've found this is the basis of the addictive relationship. We move from relationship to relationship with the impossible idea that someone else will make things better for us. In the addictive relationship, we're drawn into the relationship from need, not from choice.

Two Ticks, No Dog

Some popular Christian marriage counselors use a visual to illustrate the destructiveness of two very needy people in a relationship. The counselors compare the needy couple to ticks, bothersome parasites that live by sucking blood from a warm-blooded animal. Dogs are favorite targets for them. Ticks will bury their heads into a canine and live there, happily feeding for however long they choose unless forcibly removed. And ticks are not easy to remove.

An addictive relationship between two individuals arrested in their development is strikingly similar to the relationship between two ticks, minus the dog and feeding on each other. The man and the woman, both self-centered and reacting from the pain of their wounds, drain the energy from the partner. Each is frantic for a life-giving source, but the person chosen has nothing to give and is looking for the same help.

When we're wounded in life, we look for someone we believe will manage our unidentified needs, but we're inevitably attracted to a fellow energy-sucker with similar wounds.

The Playground

Imagine a nine-year-old child in a romantic relationship with a 30-year-old. It's an absurd, perverse idea that we cringe at. But with this in mind, we can understand how a man or woman who still acts nine years old will seek a partner whose maturity level is at approximately the same age but who is really 30 years old.

How does a nine-year-old boy get the attention of a girl he has a crush on? He throws a rock at her, kicks her, or chases her. In adulthood the wounded man, when angry and unable to explain what he needs, will communicate the same way. When the woman fails to meet the need, he resents her and his need to be with her. Unfortunately, when we're in this situation, we can't recognize our own needs, and thus our partner cannot fulfill them.

Like small children, we who are wounded communicate unnamed needs with unacceptable behavior: tantrums, explosive anger, and fits. When others react negatively to our unacceptable behavior, we blame them. We can't figure out what's wrong with us, but at the same time, we can't handle the rejection that may come if we try to find out the truth.

Instead, we toss out accusatory statements like "She

doesn't love me enough," "He doesn't meet my needs," and "She's not there for me." The relationship loses all energy, and the frustration escalates. If we're healthy, we could accept what our partner offers—but we can't. We constantly challenge the other person to prove himself or herself. Nothing ever gets resolved. We have no ability to handle our conflicts with maturity and love.

Emotional Clams

A strange dichotomy of this is that we're willing to struggle a great deal in our addictive relationships because the fight is familiar, and we know how to cope with it. We're used to using these methods to get what we think we want. But real resolution requires vulnerability and opens the doors for rejection. So we never get down to the truth. We remain afraid of being vulnerable and tear down the emotional walls. Unfortunately, if and when we do reveal our feelings in addictive relationships, our openness is used against us as a weapon in the heat of battle.

During a relationship I was in while divorced from my wife, my girlfriend shared her past with me. Later, in moments of anger, I used that information to degrade her. I compounded her misery and then forced her back behind her walls. By my calling her names and bringing up her mistakes, she learned once again not to trust.

An old tale recommends that if you really want to bear your soul, drive into the desert and find a big lop-eared jackrabbit. Pour your heart out to him. Cry on his shoulder and tell him everything you ever wanted to express: your pain, your fears, your weaknesses, and your failures. Then, just before you go back to your car, shoot him.

When we're in addictive relationships, we're willing to give only a percentage of commitment and vulnerability in exchange for enough to make each relationship worth the investment. It ends up being a pittance of real love and respect, won at the cost of great pain we give to each other.

What happens? Unable to make a true emotional commitment, we establish a counterfeit emotional bond based on sexuality rather than on relationship. Two wounded people go directly from the gift of attraction to a sexual relationship with no foundation. They're not friends or really even acquaintances.

Many times in this type of relationship we want out, but we can't get out. It's easier to stay. We would rather bear continuous pain as a couple instead of facing the pain of rejection and possibly being alone. This develops into the condition of codependency.

The Rescuers

A wealthy Texas businessman's father died when he was seven years old. His family, wanting to shield him from the pain of losing his father, never explained to him about death or why his father was suddenly gone. The boy told his school friends that his daddy took a trip to Europe and would someday be back.

As an adult, the businessman dated several women who were educated, intelligent, and balanced, yet he wasn't comfortable with any of them. He began looking for a woman who was hurting and found a girl in her 20s. He married her, wanting to rescue her from her pain. In his mind, this young woman would not leave him like a healthy, balanced woman might. She wouldn't leave him as his father did, because she was wounded and needed him.

He became the father and caretaker in his relationship and didn't realize that no woman can sustain a marriage to a man she sees as her father.

In time, this wife returned to college and eventually left her husband for a much older professor. The businessman dealt with the abandonment the same way he had dealt with his father's death—by denying it. "She'll be back," he told others.

In this kind of addictive relationship, we expect our partner to "fix" us. We look for a person who will erase our wounds. For example, my relationship with my wife remained frozen in time: I forced her to deal with issues that stemmed from long before I met her. She didn't even know about these issues, but she had to deal with their results in the abuse and anger I cast at her.

Like that businessman, a rescuer avoids his or her personal wounds by focusing on someone else. These people tell themselves, "If I can help this person, I'll have value. He [She] won't reject or leave me, because I take care of him [her], and he [she] needs me."

The Rescuer's Checklist

Here's a checklist of questions to ask yourself to see if you're playing the role of a rescuer in your relationships:

- Is it hard for you to take time for yourself and have fun?
- Do you supply words for your partner if he or she hesitates?
- Do you set boundaries for yourself and then break them?
- Do you believe you're responsible to make your partner happy?
- Do you enjoy lending a shoulder for your partner to cry on?
- Do you believe your partner is not sufficiently grateful for your help?
- Do you take care of your partner more than you take care of yourself?
- Do you find yourself interrupting when your partner is talking?
- Do you watch for clues for ways to be helpful to your partner?
- Do you make excuses emotionally or mentally for your partner's behavior?
- Do you do more than your share—work harder than your partner?
- When your partner is unsure or uncomfortable about doing something, do you do it for him or her?
- Do you give up doing things because your partner wouldn't like it?
- Do you find yourself thinking that you really know what's best for your partner?
- Do you think your partner would have serious difficulty getting along without you?

- Do you use the word "we" and then find out you don't have your partner's consent?
- Do you stop yourself by thinking how your partner would react if you did or said something?
- Is it hard for you not to respond to anyone who seems hurting or needing help?
- Do you find yourself being resented when you were only trying to be helpful?
- Do you find yourself giving advice that's not welcome or accepted?

If you answer many of these questions with a yes, you're probably forcing yourself into the mold of a rescuer and might be in a codependent relationship.

But how do you tell the difference between rescuing and merely being helpful and concerned? Consider these contrasts:

- *The helper*—listens or requests. A balanced person in a relationship is not always looking for a way to establish priority in his or her partner's life. The helper listens more than he or she talks.
- *The rescuer*—does most of the talking and is angry when his or her counsel is not accepted and acted upon.
- *The helper*—will let the partner stand on his or her own two feet, recognize his or her own needs, and ask for help.
- *The rescuer*—tries to read the mind of others and fulfill needs before being asked, even surprising friends by fulfilling their needs in an attempt to make their friendship indispensable.
- *The helper*—presents an offer.
- *The rescuer*—doesn't first see if his or her assistance is welcome.
- *The helper*—gives what's needed.
- *The rescuer*—gives more and much longer than needed.
- *The helper*—checks for results. He or she looks to see if his or her goals are met, will solve problems, and will use suggestions.
- *The rescuer*—doesn't check results, feels good when

the idea is accepted, and feels rejected when suggestions are turned down.

If we try to find partners who will fix us instead of real-
izing that such a mind-set is a serious problem, we'll encounter the same frustrations again and again. If we're rescuers and are searching for another wounded person to
"fix," we'll never ask the tough questions, confront our own
wounds, and find personal wholeness. Rescuers will also repeat the pattern of seeking unhealthy relationships.

Negative, Positive, or None of the Above

Psychologists have found that it takes seven positive
statements to equal the impact of one negative statement.
What is the first word that children hear? By the time we're
two or three years of age, we've heard the word "no" more
than 40,000 times. By the time we're 16, we've heard
173,000 negative statements about ourselves. On the average, well tell ourselves 16 negative statements per day. If we
really listen, we can catch ourselves making statements
like "I did such a dumb thing," "I'm so stupid," or "I can't do
anything right today." Like stories from the newspaper, we
begin to believe our own negative press, and it affects how
we see ourselves.

Our self-esteem is directly tied to how we make decisions. If we don't like or trust ourselves, we'll not like or
trust our decisions. As a result, our decisions will be made
by indecision. We debate, argue, and stall until circumstances finally settle the issues. Most of the time, a decision
made by indecision is a bad decision.

We often can't make a decision because we can't see the
whole picture and realize the consequences of our actions.
It's like riding a train with the bridge out two miles ahead.
You know the bridge is out, but you can't get off the train in
time. Not until the train begins plummeting into the gorge
do you realize, "A mile ago I really should have jumped off of
this train." We can see what's going to happen, but we're
locked in childish behavior, looking for someone to stop the
train. We can't even decide to jump off the train by ourselves.

This is how we're drawn into addictive relationships. We

don't know what we need. We think of ourselves as worthless, and we fear rejection. We refuse to decide to commit or not commit, to love or not love, to stay with someone or not. Suddenly we're locked into a destructive relationship, praying that someone will save us. But the real problem is that we can't jump to the ground of commitment, love and loyalty.

My life illustrates this statement. I could never make decisions in relationships, and I would hang around without a real commitment until it was too late. The last relationship I had made me realize I was hooked on the relationship. I knew the relationship was over because of my feelings of guilt and shame, but I was so addicted to my partner and the thought of losing her that I couldn't decide one way or the other.

I cried out to God, *You're going to have to deliver me from this relationship, because I'll die in it! I'm so weak!*

This woman had previously threatened me with legal action over my abusive behavior, so we both knew the relationship was over; however, neither of us could leave. When she came home that last night, I was so angry that I started a fight, and it escalated to physical abuse and my threatening her life. She ended up in a shelter for battered women, and I ended up in therapy with the charge of attempted murder hanging over my head. God used these horrendous circumstances to make me realize that the violence was *my* issue and *mine* alone.

Shame and Guilt

Our wounds form a shame-based mentality which destroys relationships, self-knowledge, and hope—and eventually destroys *us*. Look at the difference between guilt and shame again.

The shame base says, "I have no options, and I'm locked into a course of action." Guilt says, "I can be accountable for my behavior, and I can change." Shame says, "I *am* a mistake; I'm no good." Guilt says, "I *made* a mistake, yet I have value as a creation of God."

God offers us a guilt base founded in the truth that helps us. Once we recognize what we've done wrong, the guilt base helps us become accountable and responsible for our wrong-doing. We learn, grow, and change with a world of possibilities lying in front of us. Shame is only an endless cycle of hopelessness, despair, and repeating the same mistakes.

God intends for us to live in a guilt-based environment. We recognize the behavior is wrong, but we can choose to change. God knows where we're headed, and He can lead us to full hope and joy if we obey.

If we're shame-based, however, we often gravitate toward people bearing the same type of pain, others who struggle with their sense of value and control. Other wounded people are more likely to accept us, because they also see themselves as without value.

To escape this cycle, we must realize that we do have value and that we *can* move ahead. We're worthy of being loved and of being a part of a healthy relationship with someone who is healthy.

The religious community was prepared to stone the adulteress when Jesus stepped in (John 8:3-11). Jesus told the woman to "Go, and sin no more" (v. 11). He saw her value despite what she had done. In a shame-based relationship, we can't see the person's value. We simply see him or her as wrong and worthy of being stoned. But in a world where guilt is possible and can be forgiven, we see the value of the person in spite of his or her behavior.

Value in Christ

We've all heard that Jesus died for us. When we're wounded, we can't accept this as truth, because we can't get past the idea that we're flawed. We reason that if anyone knew the truth about us, they most certainly wouldn't love us.

Nonetheless, in spite of our actions, our behavior, and our shame, Jesus saw that we have value. He died for Paul Hegstrom. He died for you. When we begin seeing value in ourselves and in other people, we can break the cycle of shame, anger and violence. We can mature in spite of our wounds and begin to seek healthy relationships, because we realize that we do deserve them. We can see the worth of Jesus' sacrifice for us.

In the early years of our ministry, a prostitute who was also involved in drugs and dealing them went through our program and began to attend church. As she came to realize that no matter what she had done God still loved her, she accepted Christ. She moved out of the area, lived with her godly parents for a while, and got involved in the Church. She met a wonderful man, married him, and developed real wholeness as a person. Today she's a happy wife and mother.

We also ministered to a couple who had both lived in immorality. They went through the program and put their marriage back together. They found the Lord and got involved in a church. About a year later, she discovered she had contracted terminal cancer. Her husband was gentle and caring, staying home in a hospice situation. He told me afterward, "We really fell in love and found a relationship with Christ because of the Life Skills program. She found her value and acceptance in Christ. When she was dying, the last day, she asked me to get the Life Skills book. I asked why, and she said she wanted to brush up on it because she was about to meet Jesus and she wanted to thank him so much for loving her."

God loves us and wants the best for our lives. He wants us to be healthy, balanced, and whole. He also wants us to be in healthy relationship with a loving spouse.

This is the kind of hope I want you to have. Health is possible!

8
MARRIED . . .
AND IT STILL
ISN'T RIGHT

A friend recently asked why many books, movies, and television programs end with a wedding. She wanted to know what happened after the loving couple exchanged their vows. She was curious to know whether their love remained faithful and strong beyond the flowers and wedding presents.

Most of our popular romances come to the thrilling conclusion of a couple deciding to spend their lives together. With very few exceptions, most Shakespearean comedies end in marriage. Classic fairy tales, even the dark tales, often include weddings. Since the time we were children, we've read of brave heroes, knights in shining armor, and beautiful heroines riding white horses off into the sunset together. We don't want to hear about the problems of work, in-laws, kids, or carpools.

William Goldman says his father used to read S. Morgenstern's book *The Princess Bride* to him, and he would finish the story with "And they lived happily ever after"— which is how most us would want to hear it. In Goldman's abridged version of the satirical swashbuckling story, he says his father was protecting him from Morgenstern's true ending, which was not so "happily ever after."

Those of us who were wounded in our childhood drag into marriage the same sack of problems and pain we carried as single adults. We may have been able to hide the baggage long enough to distract our spouse from noticing its size or power, but soon our wounds surface in our new marriage. The partner we hoped would meet our nameless needs faces a new series of tests. As our frustration and anger grows, we push every boundary. Life together quickly becomes more of a nightmare than a fairy tale. Because this is the way we've always done things, we honestly don't know any other way to live.

When Judy and I married for the first time, she looked forward to our having a happy life together. She didn't think I would hit her ever, much less the second day into our marriage. In our courtship she never saw how quickly my rage would turn to manipulation, so this came as a complete surprise. When she tried to get close to me emotionally, I began to feel too vulnerable. I would hit her, lash out, or say something degrading until she backed away. She could never create any intimacy in that environment. I attacked her value, her self-worth, and her physical appearance. These lies soon became truth to her. I told her no one else would want her, and she believed me.

Why does this happen? In unhealthy relationships, we quickly fall into a pattern of codependency, expecting a partner to complete our unresolved problems. We agree to attend counseling, but only so we can point a finger at our spouse and the therapist can fix *his* or *her* problems. We have no foundation or stability, so we both fear abandonment and cling together. We are two ticks sucking life from each other with no dog in sight to save us.

In the Life Skills program, we don't counsel couples together until each person has spent almost one year of individual counseling in our program. We seek to deal with the behavior from each partner's wounds—which, in a perfect world, should have been dealt with before either person ever dated anyone, let alone each other. We work with the individual first.

The Marital Bond

Women are usually more emotionally driven than sexually driven, whereas men are more sexually driven than emotionally driven. When the two come together emotionally and bond, they become whole, completely connected to each other. When they have bonded emotionally, their sexuality will respond in a healthy manner. They will both look forward to each aspect of their relationship and grow together. However, a husband without an emotional bond to his wife will see her as someone who sleeps with him, cleans the house, takes care of the children, and works—he won't see her as a real, living emotional person.

When the couple has a sexual bond without an emotional bond, the wife's sexual desire will start to diminish within the first 30 to 36 months of marriage. They become roommates rather than husband and wife.

My Needs, Your Needs, and Our Needs

Men, it's time we admit to the truth. We are as dumb as a bag of rocks when it comes to reading a woman's mind. We've all been in those arguments in which our wives storm, "You know what you did!" Honestly—we don't. Women, you need to admit that you don't understand us any better than we understand you.

A comical E-mail is often forwarded from computer to computer about a couple on a date. After the woman mentions that they've been dating for six months, the reader sees how both the man's and the woman's individual thoughts go in different directions from that statement.

As the silence between the two grows, the woman worries that her boyfriend might see her comment as a need for a deeper commitment, and she begins examining her desire to be in a serious relationship. The man recalls that six months ago he had his tires rotated and silently wonders if he should take his car into the shop for maintenance. In the middle of his mental auto diagnostic, the woman blurts out that she has no need to be rescued by a knight in shining armor on a white horse and suggests the couple spend some time apart. Overwhelmed by her assertion and very unsure of where her decision came from, the man humbly agrees. Several weeks pass. While playing racquetball with a mutual friend, the man asks, "Did Gwen ever mention her horse to you?"

Even in a normal marriage, both partners lack mind-reading ability and can't read the other person's needs. As a result, they pursue a normal course of action: they ask what those needs are and then try to meet them. In a wounded relationship, the partners take a different course of action: they childishly manipulate each other, react badly, become angry, and begin to accuse, berate, and so on. It turns into continual chaos.

One evening in one of our classes, a man had an emotional breakthrough. His wife was in the women's class upstairs in the building. After class, she met him in the parking lot but didn't realize that he had had a tough evening and wanted a hug. He needed to be validated.

By the time they reached the car, they were screaming at each other. In frustration, he pinned her against the side of the car. Drawn by the commotion, I intervened and asked him, "What's going on here? What are you feeling right now?"

"Well, I don't know. I'm mad. I'm angry," the man answered.

"Does rejection have anything to do with it?"

"Yeah, everything to do with it," he admitted.

"What do you want? If you could have anything you want from her right now, what would it be?"

"I just want a hug."

"Why didn't you ask her for it?"

He was getting ready to attack her because she wouldn't hug him. But she couldn't read his mind. She couldn't see through his anger and frustration to know he needed a hug. He stood crying like a small child while she comforted and validated him. It's a basic principle of health and marriage: communicate. Say what you want. Don't expect someone else to figure it out for you.

How We Act When Things Aren't Right

When we're lacking an emotional bond, disappointed by unmet needs and carrying unresolved hurts, our frustration must find an outlet. Here are some behaviors that block intimacy between a husband and wife and become a disheartening nightmare in the relationship. He or she

- blocks love and intimacy

- denies problems
- constantly complains
- has no boundaries
- considers life only an existence
- must prove self
- is performance oriented
- internalizes
- is isolated/irritable
- is lonely/distrustful
- feels suicidal/hopeless
- is fearful/anxious
- has a hostile sense of humor
- is nagging/critical
- is defensive and provoking
- is angry/jealous
- has frequent crying spells
- controls others/situations/circumstances
- exhibits no self-control
- is manipulative
- allows no emotions

These behaviors are consistent between a wounded couple in a home where physical abuse is *not* present. The Power and Control Wheel [*Figure 8-A*] provides a detailed look at the damage in a situation in which domestic violence occurs. My book *Angry Men and the Women Who Love Them* deals specifically with domestic violence in further detail.

Childish Behavior Isn't Cute at 40

Earlier, we examined behavior that was normal for healthy development in early childhood. In a growing child, this behavior is how we learn. In a 40-year-old adult, the behavior is inappropriate. Let's look at how the same early-childhood behavior surfaces in the marriage of wounded adults.

We don't know where we end and our partner begins. In adulthood, this childish behavior may surface in identity issues. We see our partner as part of our identity. We see ourselves as having value only when people respond to us.

FIGURE 8-A

VARIETIES OF ABUSE

There don't have to be bruises for there to be abuse.

Changing the form of the abuse is not the same as stopping the abuse.

Physical abuse: any touch not given in love, respect, or dignity.

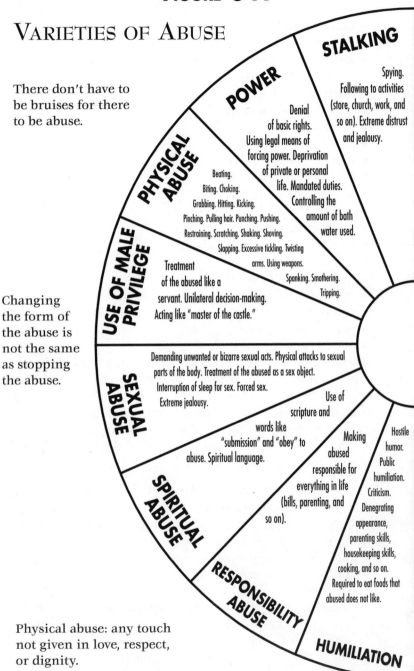

STALKING
Spying. Following to activities (store, church, work, and so on). Extreme distrust and jealousy.

POWER
Denial of basic rights. Using legal means of forcing power. Deprivation of private or personal life. Mandated duties. Controlling the amount of bath water used.

PHYSICAL ABUSE
Beating. Biting. Choking. Grabbing. Hitting. Kicking. Pinching. Pulling hair. Punching. Pushing. Restraining. Scratching. Shaking. Shoving. Slapping. Excessive tickling. Twisting arms. Using weapons. Spanking. Smothering. Tripping.

USE OF MALE PRIVILEGE
Treatment of the abused like a servant. Unilateral decision-making. Acting like "master of the castle."

SEXUAL ABUSE
Demanding unwanted or bizarre sexual acts. Physical attacks to sexual parts of the body. Treatment of the abused as a sex object. Interruption of sleep for sex. Forced sex. Extreme jealousy.

SPIRITUAL ABUSE
Use of scripture and words like "submission" and "obey" to abuse. Spiritual language.

RESPONSIBILITY ABUSE
Making abused responsible for everything in life (bills, parenting, and so on).

HUMILIATION
Hostile humor. Public humiliation. Criticism. Denegrating appearance, parenting skills, housekeeping skills, cooking, and so on. Required to eat foods that abused does not like.

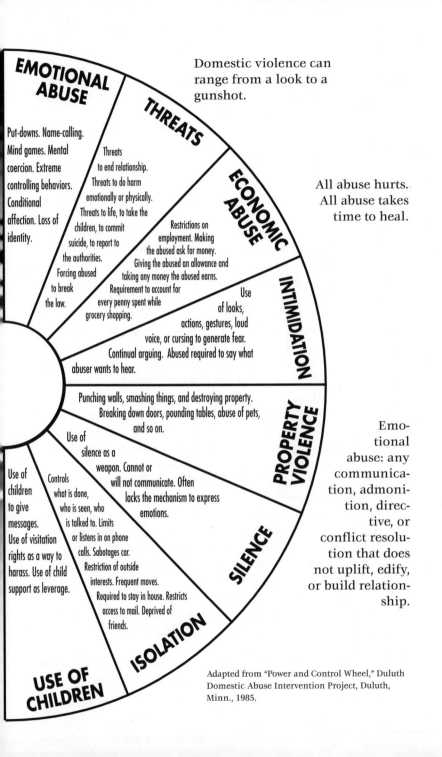

Domestic violence can range from a look to a gunshot.

All abuse hurts. All abuse takes time to heal.

Emotional abuse: any communication, admonition, directive, or conflict resolution that does not uplift, edify, or build relationship.

EMOTIONAL ABUSE

Put-downs. Name-calling. Mind games. Mental coercion. Extreme controlling behaviors. Conditional affection. Loss of identity.

THREATS

Threats to end relationship. Threats to do harm emotionally or physically. Threats to life, to take the children, to commit suicide, to report to the authorities. Forcing abused to break the law.

ECONOMIC ABUSE

Restrictions on employment. Making the abused ask for money. Giving the abused an allowance and taking any money the abused earns. Requirement to account for every penny spent while grocery shopping.

INTIMIDATION

Use of looks, actions, gestures, loud voice, or cursing to generate fear. Continual arguing. Abused required to say what abuser wants to hear.

PROPERTY VIOLENCE

Punching walls, smashing things, and destroying property. Breaking down doors, pounding tables, abuse of pets, and so on.

SILENCE

Use of silence as a weapon. Cannot or will not communicate. Often lacks the mechanism to express emotions.

ISOLATION

Controls what is done, who is seen, who is talked to. Limits or listens in on phone calls. Sabotages car. Restriction of outside interests. Frequent moves. Required to stay in house. Restricts access to mail. Deprived of friends.

USE OF CHILDREN

Use of children to give messages. Use of visitation rights as a way to harass. Use of child support as leverage.

Adapted from "Power and Control Wheel," Duluth Domestic Abuse Intervention Project, Duluth, Minn., 1985.

An individual arrested in development at this stage in childhood may also show a tendency to resent the person he or she is so dependent on. This is the partner who feels and says, "I hate you—don't leave me."

We don't know where we end and the world begins. When our spouse is the base for exploration, as our parents were before, other relationships are free to be explored. We know this is entirely wrong in a marriage, but we see our spouse as a safe place, and we want to experience the excitement of the world.

If we can't see it, it doesn't exist. In this relationship, privacy is stripped away. When we're a wounded partner, we crush, consume, and turn our spouse into a play object. The spouse becomes as part of the furnishings or part of our inventory.

We disrupt the world to get our way. We want what we want when we want it. We see ourselves as the center of the universe and will do whatever we can to get our way. Our impulse control is low. As adults needing validation, we act out when people don't respond to us. We can be controlling and manipulative.

We engage in parallel play. We all know married couples who have separate checking accounts, closets, and shelves for their books and CDs. They've never really merged their lives together. They may have a hidden fear that this relationship won't last and thus fear losing their stuff. Where true emotional bonding has occurred, everything is shared.

Emotionally childish, we aren't able to deal with loss. For example, a husband owns a large wrench-and-socket set but loses one piece. Now he sees that whole set as ruined. Likewise, if his wife leaves or gets counseling, the whole marriage is ruined, because he sees the relationship as out of his control. When a spouse gets help or leaves, a wounded person feels he or she has lost the spouse, because to that point the spouse has been a possession and part of the wounded person's inventory.

Never being able to let go of ownership can lead to dangerous situations, even stalking. The spouse will do anything to make up the loss: lose his or her job, spend all the couple's money, destroy relationships. We can't maintain anything, and we can focus only on what we've lost.

In a healthy, mature adult relationship we can gain perspective on loss and see the bigger picture. As we seek healing and grow emotionally, we can focus on our work and priorities, set goals, and realize what it takes to develop thriving relationships.

We deal in compartmental thinking. In my first marriage to Judy, I could go home to her while having an affair with another woman. I put the affair in a box, walked out of the box, closed the lid, and went home to be a part of my family. In my immaturity, I could compartmentalize everything in my life. I wanted a wife to take care of me, and a girlfriend to be a trophy. I never understood the pain of betrayal. Those of us who have been wounded in childhood will justify it, explain it, and refuse to understand why such behavior is wrong, unacceptable, and must stop.

Authority of Our Partners

If we're dealing with childhood wounds, we fear authority, because those in authority at the time of our wounding weren't able to protect us or to help us cope. As a result, we become our own authorities, defying anyone to place boundaries on us. We move from not respecting the authority of a parent to not respecting our teachers, our mentors, our bosses, our pastors, and finally our mate. We see our mate as an authority, not a team player.

In our first marriage, Judy might say, "Honey, my parents are coming for a couple of days, and I need some money for groceries. How much money do we have in the bank?"

I would react by snapping at her, "It's none of your business what I have in the bank!"

Then I would give her some money (not necessarily enough) to feed our family of five plus the two guests. Rather than talking to her about the checking account and telling her that I trusted her judgment, I exerted my control.

Remember that, like children, our perception is everything to us. Our spouse may truly be trying to be a team player and a real partner, but we perceive his or her actions as a threat to our position of control. *Our* childish perception of the situation governs everything.

Attacking Problems Together

Judy and I have been remarried now for 17 nonviolent years. We have chosen to work at rebuilding trust, work on our friendship, and firmly establish emotional intimacy. We've learned to define our problems together and attack the problems rather than each other. We've also learned that the value of the relationship is always greater than the conflict at hand. This means sometimes calling "time out." We do whatever we need to do to resolve the conflict, and we remember that the value of the person in our relationship is always greater than the problem.

How have we reached this point? By becoming vulnerable, admitting fears and hidden experiences, and forgiving—the kind of things I could not do as a wounded adult in our earlier marriage.

Setting Boundaries

When we're wounded, we often consider forgiveness as a means of returning to the same problem or situation, re-establishing the same relationship, and repeating the same destructive patterns. This wasn't God's intention for forgiveness. Forgiveness acts as a catalyst for *change*.

In the Bible, Jesus set boundaries and created an amazing example for us to follow. In Luke 18:18-26, the rich young ruler asked Jesus how he could have eternal life. Jesus provided the boundaries. He said, "You must give up everything and follow Me. Take it or leave it. This is My way" (v. 22, author's paraphrase)

After the ruler's rejection, Jesus didn't chase him down the road, saying, "Wait a minute—let's talk this out! We really do need another person in the Kingdom!" He simply let the young man go his own way.

In the wounded relationship, we can't simply forgive without expecting real change to take place. Every action has a consequence, and while we can forgive unacceptable behavior, we don't want to repeatedly fall victim to it. Consequences must lead to change. We have a right to set boundaries and expect them to be respected.

Every marriage that wants to get beyond codependency and addictive behavior must call for real change when forgiveness is offered.

When One-Half of the Whole Is Healed

What happens in a relationship in which one partner is wounded and the other healthy? For a wife in this situation, I counsel her to move on and develop her own character, find her balance, and realize her value. Her new life doesn't shove her wounded partner out. She includes him if he wants to be included, but she refrains from reacting wrongly to his behavior and allowing him to drag her down emotionally.

In time, a wounded husband will respect that. However, he will fear that she will leave him because of it. This opens up two options for him: either work on his own issues or get left behind in his immaturity. I believe the best thing we can do is move forward in growth, grace, and mercy, while at the same time requiring our wounded partner to get help and deal with his or her issues realistically and biblically.

In this regard, as stated earlier, I believe that a healthy husband or wife can never counsel his or her wounded spouse. It always takes a third party.

Building Trust

When Judy and I decided to remarry, I was a changed person. However, she couldn't trust me. She was right not to trust me. I had told Judy a hundred times in our first marriage that I would never hurt her again. I broke promise after promise—sometimes within an hour of making the vow. After God changed my life, I meant business, but she needed to know she was safe. How could she learn to trust my word?

In our program we have what we call "Ninety days of

shut up and duck." Our spouses need to regain our trust, so for three months we will help them start to trust us by us listening and responding in love, no matter how they might react. Trust is difficult to establish under any conditions. But when the wounded spouse has broken trust so many times, he or she must rebuild it by learning to listen and love first before making his or her own needs known.

I particularly remember one couple from New Hampshire whom we counseled. The man was very rigid and self-centered, controlling and manipulative. She couldn't express any feelings. We got him into this program and told him that he had to let her say anything to him. He could not respond except at the end by saying, "I'm beginning to understand how you feel."

They did this. For 30 to 45 days, the wife was afraid to say anything, and she acted much like a pressure cooker—exploding now and then. But as she found her husband responding to her in this new way, she began to realize she was safe and could talk to him. At the end of 90 days, he found he knew her better than he ever had in his life. Much of what he assumed she was trying to say earlier in their relationship now came out in the truth. He began to truly love her through this process.

How do we reach complete healing in this way? We'll look at that in the pages ahead.

THE
WOUNDED
AT WORK

9

In the 1970s television sitcom *WKRP in Cincinnati,* the job of selling radio ads and raising revenue for the struggling rock station fell to comical character Herb Tarlek. He always dressed in tacky plaids and tossed crude come-ons at Jennifer, the receptionist.

Herb typified a combination of false bravado and annoying ambition. He was the type of guy you might encounter at a party and then whisper to a friend, "What's up with that guy?"

When I was in my mid-30s, during the time I was fighting my own behavior, I worked for a large radio station in the Midwest. I was Herb Tarlek in the flesh. Immediately I told my new boss that I thought he should know that something was wrong with me. I had a character flaw and sometimes felt as if I were retarded. I also let him know I would work for him for two or three years and outsell any other salesman. My advertising billing, I announced, would be higher than those of all the other salesmen combined.

Creative and persistent, I would have two or three highly productive days during the week. I would pitch wild advertising ideas and wow my customers with how I planned to make radio advertising work for them. I would grab large chunks of their marketing budget in just one meeting.

The rest of the week I would battle insecurity—feeling exactly like a small child playing "grown-up" in an adult's world. Every other day I became physically sick at the possibility that I might be rejected the next time I headed into a meeting.

This pattern would occur in every job I held. After a couple of years, my employers would see through the juggling act that hid my anger and mood swings, and I would move on to another job.

The wounds of our childhood affect each facet of our lives, not merely our relationships. As we head off to work every morning, we drag behind us our growing sack of frustrations and behaviors we have carried since our wound. We may hide the sack, but we can't hide the survival techniques we use to keep ourselves safe.

The Mask Is Back

For the wounded person, the mask never really goes away. We protect ourselves by showing different personalities when we're with different people. We create our pseudopersonality to meet the expectations of important people in our lives— we're certain they'll reject us if they see our defectiveness. When we were younger, our parents and perhaps some of our teachers were those important people. As we have moved into adulthood, the circle has widened to include our friends, our church community, and our employers.

Our careers create a vast area of vulnerability, because a failure in our career reflects directly on our abilities. If our coworkers don't see the "real" or core us, it's harder for us to be hurt by them. The mask protects our vulnerability.

Self-preservation is the reason it's possible, even likely, for workaholic and apathetic employees to be masking their wounds. The workaholic is performance oriented and connects his or her worth with how much he or she can accomplish. *Staying alive and being valuable means I must keep doing and achieving,* thinks the workaholic.

On the other hand, a wounded apathetic individual who wears an *I couldn't care less about this job* attitude as a badge of honor is protecting his or her core by adopting a different work ethic. By devaluing the job, the employer, and coworkers, this individual survives by not letting the job devalue him or her. *I can't be hurt by this job or anyone associated with it, because I just don't care enough about it,* thinks an apathetic employee.

Both perfectionism and apathy mask the core. When we look at the life of a serial killer like Ted Bundy, we can clearly see the difference between the core personality and the mask. Friends and coworkers would say Bundy was a model citizen, charismatic and engaging. Yet at his core, he was angry and turned to violent acts and murder.

Holding onto the wounds of our childhood, we will fight to keep the mask in place. When we interview for a job, we put our best foot forward. Our perception is that we are defective at our core. Accordingly, we show the great side of our personality in a job interview. The employer hires us based on the appeal of that personality.

Life Skills research demonstrates that within six to seven months after taking a new job, our core personality will become dominant. Anger bleeds into the workplace. We need to be noticed. We are not team players. The self-centeredness and control starts to appear. As we grow older, the sack of anger, wounds, and trauma we're dragging has become too large to constantly hide, even for self-preservation. The mask slips, and the childish behavior from our wounds—added to the survival techniques we use to manage our pain—are revealed on the job.

Childish Traits at Work

As with the workaholic and the apathetic employee, we each reveal reactive behavior from our childhood wounds in different ways and to varying degrees. Some of us can be highly productive, ambitious, driven, and even overachieving on the job. Some of us battle just to get out of bed each morning and make a passionless attempt to get through the day. In our hearts, we may be afraid of success, and we certainly fear failure. We distrust authority and wrestle with being team players in the workplace. However, if and when we acknowledge our childish actions in the workplace, we realize the benefit of confronting our behavior, and through that beginning the healing process will radically change everything for us. The following are some observations on some of these childish traits at work.

Can't take directives and creates systems within the system. We become our own authority when we lose respect for the authority that didn't protect us when we were wounded. In a work environment, we still won't respect authority. We will find a way to create our own system within the system so we can continue to be our own boss.

For example, by outselling others, I convinced my boss to let me do things my own way, and I would continue to make large profits for him. "Force me to work like the other guys, and I'll probably be worthless," I said smugly. I hated the structure of a time clock, sales meetings, daily reports, and coming back to the office at 4:30. Accountability was something to battle.

Untrustworthy and steals ideas. People in the office who carry childhood wounds may seem to have great ideas but cannot bring them to fruition. They also may be sneaky and underhanded. They justify stealing ideas. A boss will find it almost impossible to create a loyal, long-term team with employees who are wounded in childhood.

Entitlement. As we've grown up with wounds and losses, we may feel entitlement to certain privileges and opportunities. Our continuous "I deserve it" attitude, regardless of the situation, is often selfishly motivated. When we can't see the big picture, we don't appreciate the goals, failures, and successes of the group.

Tardiness and procrastination. Both tardiness and procrastination can be signs that we are rejecting the job before the job or our employer can reject us. If we can bend the rules most of the time, we will feel special. This feeds the need to expect more than normal people get, which makes us feel validated.

Not being a team player. If we've been wounded, we'll suffer from a low self-image until we can find healing. Working with others seems to magnify our faults. When we work on our own, people don't notice many of our mistakes. We also aren't obligated to share our successes.

After years of wearing a mask, we've developed methods

to isolate ourselves and keep people from discovering who we really are. Isolation isn't always a result of shyness or physically moving away from people. We can also create distance by using humor and charisma to deflect authentic relationships. We isolate ourselves at work, citing the following attitudes:

- "I work better on my own."
- "If I can take this part of the project and work on it separately, I can bring my findings back to the group. I think it'll save time."
- "This afternoon's meeting is mandatory so I'll be there, but they're just covering pointless topics."
- "If I had a choice, I'd be somewhere else."

Also, to make ourselves look more mature and valuable than our coworkers, we'll often create chaos and then be able to fix the chaotic situation. This makes us look like heroes.

Inability to manage anger and emotions. When the mask has slipped, all the emotions we've been juggling behind it are revealed. Often we can't keep juggling the fear, frustration, hurt, and anger. They come crashing down and manifest themselves in unprofessional manners. We lash out, make inappropriate remarks, cry sporadically, and our moods change rapidly. Mentally, we become like the proverbial bumblebee in a Mason jar.

Inability to take criticism. We see direction as critical comments directed toward our work. If my work is my identity, the directive and the criticism are aimed straight at my value:

- "If my manager says my report needs to be rewritten, I've let him down. I'm a disappointment to my boss."
- "My supervisor is on my back again. Obviously, I can't do anything right."

Inability to make decisions; tendency to project weakness. Because of our loss of value and self-esteem, we have a hard time trusting our own decisions or abilities. By playing the victim, we're less likely to try, only to fail again and reveal our inadequacies. Letting our coworkers and supervisors expect little from us, we reinforce the already poor self-image we possess; yet we tend to manipulate and control wherever we can. We can tell others what they should do, but we struggle with our own decisions.

Hidden agendas. Since our wounding occurred, we have doubted truth and fought trust and knowledge. At work, we have a hard time not reading hidden agendas into situations, and we fear the worst. We think our coworkers want to see us fail."

- "The boss's closed door can only mean she's talking with someone about my work."
- "Jan and Charles were whispering over coffee this morning. I bet they were criticizing my sales proposal. Charles is still upset that the vice-president took me to lunch last week."
- "The manager reorganized the work schedule again. I know I'm working twice as many night shifts as anyone else in the plant. That guy must hate me."

Many other signs of wounding may surface in the workplace as our minds creatively keep us in a survival mode. These behaviors all have a core. They don't arise from a vacuum. Our poor self-image is one key to our problems at work, as is the feeling of powerlessness we constantly fight. "If I could just be in control," we think, "everything would be all right."

Resentment against the boss. Most of us have been trying to gain a sense of control in our own lives since we were wounded. Something was stolen from us, and we think we need to be our own boss to make up for our loss. We're all familiar with the childish phrase that a seven-year-old will fling at an older sibling, "You're not my boss!" We're ashamed, because we know at work we shouldn't feel that way, but we do. It's a 24-hour-a-day power struggle. We often fight authority in the workplace the same way we have always fought authority. Most people will always work under figures of authority: directors, vice-presidents, managers, and mentors.

Frustrated, we will find it difficult to respect authority, and much of our behavior will result from our desire to control.

As mentioned earlier, mentoring is a popular concept

in today's workplace. This involves partnering an experienced employee with a less-experienced employee. They will work together to set goals for training, personal development, and achievement. The mentor also functions as an outlet for job-related dissatisfaction and stress. If we were wounded, our difficulty with authority will carry into a mentoring relationship. Still needing to control, we'll want to mentor our mentor.

Still at War

Some Vietnam War veterans still live in the jungle. Vivid images of death and destruction replay like a scratched record, and they can never change the scenery. To avoid living as an adult, these soldiers become isolated, because they're stuck in the war and can't move on with life.

In our wounds, we tend to take responsibility for events happening to us and around us. So many children feel responsible for their parents' divorce or separation because they're too young to recognize the bigger picture. Young men who go off to fight in a violent war at the ages of 17 or 18 wrestle with the same responsibility. The crimes they witness, and the killing they must commit, becomes a weight piled on top of that responsibility. Those soldiers will carry it around in their sack of wounds unless healing occurs.

In the 19 years of our program, we've worked with hundreds of soldiers who came home wanting to live normal lives. Yet these people are plagued not only with nightmares of battles they can't win but by behavior they don't understand. When they do understand the arrested development syndrome, they can restart the maturing process. As a result, we see lives change. Healing awaits us when we release the responsibility for situations over which we had no control.

I'm an Employer. What Can I Do?

"Where there is no vision, the people perish," reads Prov. 29:18 (KJV).

All employer-staff relationships are challenging, but how does an employer improve the working situation with a wounded employee?

An employer is not responsible for his or her employees' healing. Even for the purposes of good stewardship, he or she must do what's best for the business. In Matt. 25, Jesus' parable of the talents relates how Scripture deals with an employee who doesn't approach his work with maturity. Before leaving for a trip, the landowner gave talents (a form of money) to each of his three servants according to their ability to work and earn more. One servant received five talents, another two talents, and the third received a single talent. The first and second servants invested their talents wisely, but the third buried his in the ground. When the master returned, the servants were called to bring forward their investments. The two servants who created more wealth were rewarded. The servant who buried the talent lost everything.

What then can an employer do to help a wounded employee function? Here are several suggestions:

- *Confront him or her.* Confront the behavior that is unacceptable. In the parable, the landowner confronted the worker who buried the talent by asking him to account for the talent he was given.

- *Set boundaries.* Establish boundaries for the employee. Having the employee work within a team, under a supervisor, or in monitored situations will bring one of two results: improved behavior or the resignation of the employee. In the parable, when the landowner entrusted his property to his servants, he left the care of his business and its future with them. Expectations and trust were placed on the servants to prosper their master.

- *Emphasize consequences.* Both positive and negative consequences force a wounded individual to realize that he or she must be accountable for his or her actions. Goals met with success are the reward of knowing that the job is done well, and this builds self-esteem. Failure means that boundaries have been crossed or the work is unsatisfactory, and the result is loss of privilege or employment. "Well done, good and faithful servant!" (Matt. 25:21, 23, KJV), the landowner proclaimed to the two who invested their talents wisely.

These consequences, however, do not license an employer to damage a wounded person even further. Balance is the key for good management. John C. Bowling writes in *Grace-Full Leadership,* "When a leader must deal firmly with a difficult situation, the graceful leader is able (and willing) to separate people from the problem" (27). Jesus said in Luke 22:27, "I am among you as one who serves."

One employer I knew had an employee who was late four to five days every week. This employee was valuable, but the employer had to stuff his anger over this. I helped this employer learn to confront. After confronting the employee and validating his work, he learned that the employee was really rebelling against the company's structure. They came to terms and established that with one more time of being late, the job was terminated.

As a result, this employee began arriving 5 to 10 minutes early every day.

When we're healthy in our emotional maturity, we approach our lives and our work with a heart of service. No longer afraid to succeed or fail, we'll thrive because our priorities are right. We realize our value and appreciate the value of others. When we realize that a reason exists for our feelings and our actions and that we do what is necessary to change our behavior, we begin to release the heavy sack of pain. Job satisfaction, success, and hope for the future then become attainable goals.

10

GOD, WHERE ARE YOU?

In ancient Greek mythology, Daedalus served as a skillful inventor and designer for King Minos of Crete. Upon losing the king's favor, Daedalus and his son, Icarus, were imprisoned in a high tower. To escape, Daedalus built wings made of feathers, thread, and wax. When the wings were completed, Daedalus instructed Icarus to be very careful not to fly too high or too low because the wings were so delicate. "Keep near me, and you'll be safe," he told his son.

The two began flying when the boy began to enjoy the adventure a little too much. He began to leave his father's side and to soar up toward the sun. The increasing heat softened the wax that held the feathers together, and the feathers came off the boy's arms. He frantically fluttered his arms, but no feathers were left on them. As he cried out to his father, he fell to the sea below.

Icarus was asked to trust his father and keep his eyes fixed on him, and his father would lead him to safety. But the boy was transfixed by the sun and led away only to perish—his father watching as his son fell to the earth.

Blinded by our wounds, we struggle to see our Heavenly Father and hear Him calling to us. The world tells us to enjoy instant gratification and pleasure. Fly high *now*, it tells us. We get everything we want up front, no waiting. In contrast, God's way is growth, maturity, and stability and is based on His timing. It's a lifelong process. He wants to guide us to freedom. He wants us to live outside our prison of arrested development. The difference is that the world calls us to be childish, while God calls us to "come as a child," trusting, loving, and forgiving.

Despite God's good intentions for us, we as wounded persons don't feel we can trust Him. We're afraid to accept the blessings of the Creator of the Universe. The wounds of childhood form our view of God, and we may have built our own theology, our view of God, to justify what we can't control. We may have been raised in very religious households where we were told that sin in our lives would keep us from a rich relationship with God. Thus, we already see ourselves as damaged. We feel sinful all of the time, unconsciously responsible for circumstances and events outside our control.

When we don't understand what's bothering us, Satan will come through the back door and drive us in areas of our lives in which we feel weak. If we've ever seriously tried to serve the Lord, certain issues in our lives keep rising to the surface to defeat us. If we were asked to categorize our weaknesses, we would probably find two or three areas that are a continuous struggle for us. We fight the same issues repeatedly.

As we become exhausted from constantly losing the battles against these weaknesses, frustration and unacceptable behavior well up inside of us. Suddenly the bubble bursts, and the childish behavior is released to ruin our relationships, sabotage our careers, and lead us to doubt God. We again feel shameful and think, *What's wrong with me?* Even if we firmly believe that God is all knowing, we feel He can't possibly love us, because He sees the "real" us, naked under our masks. He sees all the behavior. He knows the games we play. In our spiritual lives, we see God as a suspended hammer waiting to fall on us.

To look at ourselves in the mirror each day, we must justify our actions. We develop our own theology, our own understanding of God. *Our perception* of God seems safer than the reality of God. It keeps Him at arm's length, and we don't have to face the truth about ourselves.

Fear of God's Truth

Rom. 1:18-20 declares, "God shows His anger from heaven against all sinful, evil men *who push away the truth from them.* For the truth about God is known to them instinctively; God has put this knowledge into their hearts. Since earliest times, men have seen the earth and sky and all God made, and have known of his existence and great eternal power. So they will have no excuse [when they stand before God at Judgment Day]" (TLB, emphasis added)

The author of Romans, the apostle Paul, then details an extensive list of behaviors that are symptomatic of direct rebellion to truth, all covered in that first chapter. Verse 25 reads, "They exchanged the truth of God for a lie, and worshipped and served created things rather than the Creator—who is forever praised."

If we've been wounded, we can tie the loss of respect for ourselves to our doubt of truth. After years of wearing masks and padding ourselves with protective inner justifications of our behavior, we don't want to recognize reality and what we've created as our version of truth. Recognizing the truth means confronting the wounds of our past, our pain, and our destructive behavior. That would make us feel vulnerable. The truth may mean facing trauma and patterns of abuse. The truth may mean looking at the pain we're causing our children.

Six months after becoming serious about therapy, one night I threw myself onto my floor and for over two hours screamed at God. Then I cried like a baby, moving from rage to tears and back again. After what seemed like an eternity, I became very still. My spirit was totally resigned, and I felt broken. The Holy Spirit, as clearly as if He were sitting next to me, said, "You've been crying out for wisdom, understanding, and knowledge, but you have an unteachable spirit."

Something inside clicked. For the first time, I realized the true extent to which I was set in my ways. I wanted things to go *my way,* and nothing else would do. I was forced to face the reality that regardless of how often I tried to get help, I always wanted healing to happen on my terms. My spirit didn't have any desire to be taught. For years I evaded dealing with the truth about myself, and I angrily blamed God for not bringing me to wholeness.

I turned over onto my back, faced the ceiling, and said, *God, what You see is what You get. I give it to You—my past, present, and future—because I'm hopeless.*

The great joy of grace is that God doesn't concede when we stomp our feet and whine. He doesn't respond to the pressure, force, manipulation, abuse, or control we typically use to get what we want. To "come as a child" means to come humbly, with an open mind and honest heart. It means facing the truth on *His* terms.

Mind, Body, and Spirit

In junior high school and high school, we learned complex scientific issues from those brick-weighted biology books. The back sections of the books were filled with bizarre, bright diagrams of internal organs and our necessary physical systems. One page would feature the details of our complex skeletal system, with preceding transparent pages laying the circulatory, central nervous, muscular, and endocrine systems over the skeleton. Finally we saw the skin, and that represented the whole body.

In the same way, our physical, emotional, and spiritual systems are overlaid. When the body becomes ill, we experience warning signs that affect all of our systems. A head cold will make a person irritable as well as producing a sore throat and a runny nose. We must understand that our symptoms show the deeper problem, and they affect our physical, emotional, and spiritual systems just like a physical ailment.

In the Body of Christ, the Church, we have an obligation to see the behavior as a symptom of a greater problem. It's too easy for us to pass judgment, throw stones, and claim that our friend "just isn't right with God." We must lift each other up in love and recognize that each of us has value to God. Jesus died, giving depth and meaning to every one of us. Who are we to take that away from someone who is a member of Christ's Body? How can the Church help wounded people see their importance?

No Value in Christ

One reason we may lose our motivation to walk with Christ is because of feelings of rejection. I once knew a pastor's wife who was an intercessory prayer warrior. She daily hit her knees, pouring out her heart for others. When she was diagnosed with cancer, she stood before the church and said, "Don't pray for me. I'm not worthy of God doing anything for me."

I believe this dear lady suffered from a deep fear of rejection.

Our fear of rejection is so great we spend far more energy trying to evade rejection than we would feel if we just experienced the rejection. The Bible's truth is that if we have accepted Christ, God has given us His cloak of righteousness. Whether we acknowledge our worthiness or not, He has made us worthy of acceptance. God has already given us infinite value.

In Brennan Manning's book *Abba's Child,* the author explains that the biggest lie Satan has ever convinced us of is that we're unlovely and unlovable. If we continue to reject ourselves, we'll also reject others. The Bible tells us to love our neighbors as ourselves. If we see no value in ourselves, how can we see value in others? In our rejection of all, we'll build our own value by degrading other people, and the cycle of shame repeats itself.

Trusting God and His People

By reading the New Testament, we can see that Christ ministered to each area of the people's lives he encountered. He delivered the demonic. He healed the sick. He fed them and ate with them. He worked alongside them, hugged their kids, and laughed with them. Christ built trust one person at a time.

Because of our wounds, our trust has vanished. We tell our church community, "You can spiritualize everything until the world stops turning, and I still won't believe you."

What we really mean is "If you'll make sense of my pain and will minister to my emotions, you'll be my friend. In spite of all I've said and done, can you find value in me and walk beside me?" This builds trust.

James writes in his epistle, "Confess your sins to each other and pray for each other so that you may be healed" (James 5:16). Isn't this the essence of the group dynamic—a safe place to resolve our conflicts?

Establish Boundaries

As we walk together and lay the building blocks for trust, those walking with us must establish boundaries. They must call our sin "sin" and mandate that we deal with it. They must also keep walking beside us. As they show that they recognize our value, we'll eventually trust them. We long for someone with whom we can share how we feel spiritually. When a person from our church community walks with us and validates us while expecting us to live within established boundaries, we have a spiritual mentor who has proven himself or herself to us.

By confronting our behavior, our mentor gives us the truth about ourselves. In our blossoming trust, we recognize the truth. When we begin to feel safe within our support system, we can begin to grow and mature.

We Can Change

Many years of dragging our sack full of behaviors and wound-driven emotions has formed in us a perception that "this is all there is" for us. We can never change. We can never serve Christ, we think. We're letting ourselves be robbed and deceived if we believe this lie.

God never intended for our lives to be chaotic. He has equipped us with the tools to make sense of our pain. He wants to see us healthy, productive, and reaching out to others.

Our Creator reveals in 1 Sam. 16:7 that we look on the outside of a person, but He looks on the inside. An underlying fact in both the Old and New Testaments is our need to grow and mature in each area of our lives. When we're facing the truth about ourselves for the first time in our lives, when we realize how valuable we are, when we have a trusted mentor to walk with us, then it's time to exercise our adult ability to make choices and decisions for our lives.

Paul writes in 2 Cor. 10:5, "We demolish arguments and every pretension that sets itself up against the knowledge of God, and we take captive every thought to make it obedient to Christ."

This is a choice. When we begin to choose and stick with our choices, we will give God room to work. However, He has given us the *choice*. Part of the beauty of being His creation is that He doesn't force us to change or follow Him. We must choose and live with the consequences of our choices.

Before my healing, I was a sexual addict. When I came to Christ, the fantasies and lusts didn't just instantly disappear from my life. I had to choose to think of something else.

"No, that's not allowed—that's not what I'm going to choose to think on," I would say aloud. When an impure thought came into my mind, I would shift my attention. At first, it might have taken 10 minutes for me to refocus on something positive. Then, in a few weeks, it would only take six minutes. Soon it was three minutes. After doing this continually for 30 months to bring my imagination captive, I was able to throw those thoughts away the moment they materialized.

The subconscious mind, working within the skills and within the perimeters of God's Word, is processing the software program He wrote for each of our minds. God designed our wiring to bring us back to health, balance, wholeness, and salvation—and to help us understand His plan for our lives. In Jude 24-25, the author says that it's the duty of the Holy Spirit to bring us to fulfillment, to teach us, remind us, and present us to the Father with great joy.

The challenge before us is to get into God's Word, spend time before God, and become open to His leading, which will take us down the road to maturity. When we're in crisis, however, we don't always have the patience and peace of mind to get into the Word to find the answers we need. Our minds are restless, and we can read a page 20 times without anything sinking into our hearts. We're absorbed by our problems and managing our emotions. How do we commit our decisions to heart and make them real in our lives?

Speaking Our Decisions

The average mind thinks at a speed of around 1,300 words per minute, yet we generally speak about 100 words per minute. Think about talking with someone who speaks slowly and deliberately. Don't we have an urge to encourage him or her to just "spit it out?" There's power in the spoken word. The Creator *spoke* the world into existence. He designed our minds, the ultimate computer, to respond to the spoken word as well. Our minds will bring out all the options and try to work them out. Make a decision, and then speak it aloud: "This is what I choose to do."

When we outline our options verbally, the steps we must take to put our decision into action become clearer. Evangelist Billy Graham never fails to mention to the television audience when he invites people to accept Christ as Savior, "If you've made a decision for Christ, call us or call a friend. Call someone and tell them."

In many churches, testifying to what God is doing in your life is part of your worship of Him and your spiritual growth. At times of temptation, I will say aloud, "Paul Hegstrom, this is not an option for your life." I'm making a choice. I'm bringing down the strongholds. I'm bringing captive the imagination.

Forgiveness

The Word of God tells us, "All have sinned and fall short of the glory of God" (Rom. 3:23). Jesus doesn't make a list of those who are eligible for forgiveness and those who have crossed the line. "Seventy times seven" is how many times He instructs Peter to forgive his brother (Matt. 18:22). Even after deciding to give complete control of our lives over to God, this gospel of forgiveness and love feels foreign to us. Because of our wounds, our only safety is by harboring bitterness and anger. The fact that God would forgive the perpetrator of our trauma feels unfair and wrong.

My mother's father beat her when she was eight years old. She was told never to have any children because of the injury. My birth was a difficult experience for her, and my mother held a grudge against her father for the rest of his life. In a group setting, she explained, "My father tried many times, after he found a relationship with Christ, to apologize for what he had done to me. I wouldn't let him. I thought, *He can live with what he did, and God can deal with him at the Judgment.*"

On his deathbed, my grandfather tried to talk with my mother and to clear the air between them. She refused. He died without the chance of truly reconciling with her. For 75 years, the weight of her grudge and inability to forgive caused unacceptable behavior in certain areas of her life. When she finally released the burden at 83 years of age and forgave her father, she became a different person.

God's forgiveness leads to wholeness. This did not diminish her value to God. He understood her pain. When she forgave, however, *she* understood her pain.

When we go fishing and catch "the big one," we start to reel in the big fish, and it's fighting like mad—tugging and writhing on the line. In life, the one who wounded us is the one who's fishing. We're the fish, stuck on a line we can't get free of no matter how hard we struggle. Forgiveness is the fish taking the hook out of its own mouth and swimming away. Forgiveness is what we do to set ourselves free of others' influence. Forgiveness is imperative for a new life to begin. Forgiveness is our ultimate gift to ourselves.

Cleansing

Turn on a faucet that hasn't been used for years, and put a clean, clear glass beneath it. As the dirt, debris, and junk that have collected in that pipe for several years flow out, ask yourself if you would drink that water. After you run the water for several minutes at full force, the water runs clear and clean. The force of the clean water from deep underground cleans out the dirty pipe.

This is what the Holy Spirit does in our lives. In John 14:18, 26, the Word says, "I will not leave you as orphans; I will come to you. . . . The Counselor, the Holy Spirit, whom the Father will send in my name, will teach you all things and will remind you of everything I have said to you."

Working as a powerful source, the Holy Spirit flows through us and cleanses us. Then we share Him with others. If we try to turn off the faucet and keep everything inside, we'll become stagnant. As we let God use us as a vessel, we become clean as we walk in obedience.

Choosing to live for God, forgiven and forgiving others, we prepare for a life of wholeness with God. We then enter a personal relationship more fulfilling than any human can offer.

Codependence in Christ

Here's a controversial idea: We were created for codependence. It's true. In His infinite wisdom, God created us with a God-shaped hole in which only *He* fits. We depend on Him for maturity, life, salvation, and eternal life. For every good thing, we depend on Him. He is Spirit, and if we choose to accept Him, He uses us to do His will.

I don't want to live one minute of my life without God. When I faced open-heart surgery in 1999, I made a pact with God. *God,* I said, *I'm going to spend eternity with You no matter what it takes. If You can see in Your foreknowledge something that would separate me from Your love and grace, then take me to heaven on the operating table.*

From the youth to the elderly, God's principles are about setting people free. I can't imagine one minute without serving Christ. I've chosen to become totally dependent on the Father. When we turn over our unmet needs, our pain, and the wounds of our childhood to Him, we find value, truth, and trust. He has a purpose for each of our lives, and He's depending on us to complete the vision He has for us. That's true codependence.

Looking for a Safe Place

Imagine Icarus, his wings disintegrating, falling to the

earth. Drawn upward by the captivating brilliance of the sun, he was lost. His father wanted only to lead him to a place of safety, a place beyond the high tower that imprisoned them.

Wounded, we desperately need to be freed of our emotional and spiritual prison. We want to be with God and become whole. How do we lay down our pain and seek His face, letting Him work? We're so tired of living a half-life of frustration and fear. We're ready to follow the Father into a safe place.

As a wounded person, I never understood God as a sovereign God—that He has my life under control and that I need to turn it over to him. One winter Judy and I bought a bird feeder and a bag of birdseed. It was below zero outside when I went out to set up the bird feeder. That night the birds marauded the thing. As I watched them, the Holy Spirit spoke to me: "Before the foundation of the world, I knew I was going to nudge you to buy this bird feeder so you could feed My creation. I did this so you would know that the way I care for sparrows is nothing compared to how much I care for you. As long as you walk in My ways, you can be sure you will find protection, provision, promise, and promotion in My kingdom."

It's truly wonderful to be part of God's plan for my life—and not my doing my own thing. I love that aspect of His sovereignty.

How, then, do you find that safe place in God? Let's look at it in our last chapter.

11
HEALING
THE WOUNDED

Before my recovery, I faced a possible 15 to 22 years in prison for attempting to murder my girlfriend. During that time I stumbled upon Paul's writing in 1 Cor. 13: "When I was a child, I acted, spoke, *thought*, and *reasoned* as a child, but when I grew up, I put away childish things" (author's paraphrase).

OK—this makes some sense, I thought. I could relate to acting like a child, because I spent 40 years of my life acting like a child. I talked like a child. I played like a child. I understood those things, but I couldn't comprehend *thinking* and *reasoning* like a child.

In God's unerring timing, that piece of Scripture finally sank in, and it shook me up. I was *reasoning* my life day by day like a small child. I could see situations and circumstances only from my perspective and had no concept of the "big picture." I justified my behavior in all circumstances. In the center of the universe where I sat, I expected all my needs and desires to be met. When I didn't get my way, I felt the whole world was against me.

Whereas Paul advises us in 1 Cor. 13:11 to "put away childish things" (KJV), Jesus said to the Nicodemus in Matt. 18:3, "I tell you the truth, unless you change and become like little children, you will never enter the kingdom of heaven."

What exactly is the fine line between childish *things* and *becoming* childlike? Haven't we been behaving like spoiled little children all our lives? Isn't the whole point of this book for us to grow into whole, mature adults?

Alan D. Wright writes in his book *A Childlike Heart,*

Deep down, every child knows that adults are bigger, stronger, and smarter. Children are not in charge of the world, and they know it.

That's their key to Heaven on earth.

They seldom go to bed at night worrying about what tomorrow holds. . . . Children have no concept of dread. . . . Children celebrate better because they don't have to be the best at everything. . . . Their lives are filled with wonder because they know they've seen only a small part of a very big world. Their imaginations are glorious because they don't assume that if they've never seen it, it can't happen. Their work is really play because they aren't worried about making a mistake and blowing their careers.

Adulthood is so difficult because we act like we're in charge of our own destiny. . . . Though we pretend to be masters of our world, we secretly know ourselves to be impostors (21-22).

Like playing dress-up, dragging out mom's high heels and dad's old suit, we've pretended to be adults. We've been childlike, but in a harmful way. We don't even enjoy the pleasures of being childlike as described above. In chapter 4, we looked at what elements made a positive, normal childhood. Jesus calls us to come to Him with open hearts and minds, trusting and feeling safe in His presence. Only by experiencing the safety and love found in God, with renewed childlike eyes, can we learn from Him, walk with Him, and mature to develop the character of Christ.

For healing and growth to occur, and to prepare for healthy relationships with God and those we love, we must "restart" our maturing process.

Confronting Truth

A healthy, God-designed, childlike perspective won't come easily or without cost. Between the sack of pain we've been dragging, our mask, our layers of self-protection, and denial, Satan will try to block us from the healing God wants us to experience:

- "You don't deserve to be happy."
- "You're bad."

- "No one who knows the truth about you loves you."

These perceptions to which we cling are a sinking raft of lies. Jesus said, "You will know the truth, and the truth will set you free" (John 8:32).

What *is* the truth? An incident of rejection or abuse (or a cluster of incidents) may have hijacked our emotional development when we were young. Our years of objectionable behavior and unknown, unmet needs have a root and a cause. Becoming aware that a reason exists helps us regain the knowledge we lack.

The Bible promises, and we've seen it demonstrated time and again in our 19 years in ministry, that understanding the cause of our behavior and feelings is the first step to repairing the damage caused by the wounds of our past. When we seriously ask, "Why do I act the way that I do?" and are desperate to be well, we must be prepared to confront the truth. The mind will lock up when we're traumatized. Since the behavior seems to have no source, we reason that something must be wrong with us. To understand that the behavior has a source releases the mind to tie the root (source) to the behavior, and this creates a reason. I can accept this reason. Then the mind will start to take responsibility for the unacceptable behavior if we allow it to do so. Always remember this: There's a reason for our pain but *never* an excuse for our unacceptable behavior.

If We Become Teachable

We must also pray for a teachable spirit. Many of us have been our own authority for so long that we have difficulty recognizing we aren't interested in learning what God is trying to teach us. We feel intense pain, but changing means getting onto our knees before God and those we love and admitting we don't have all the answers. We need to humbly ask to start again like a child and deal with all the learning processes we have to go through.

Guidelines for the Healing Process

Identify primary behaviors that are inappropriate and undermine dignity. This requires complete honesty. The guidance of a trusted friend or counselor is very helpful and highly recommended during this process. If we're serious about healing, we must stop pointing our fingers at others or letting ourselves be victims to our feelings of shame.

It's frightening to recognize how we have sabotaged our wholeness and happiness with our reactive behavior. But with that realization comes the ability to understand why we act the way we do and the ability to make important changes in our lives.

It's an option to find the sources of pain, but not necessary to force memories out in order to confront past issues. Digging for memories of trauma has been a controversial subject in the mental health community. Our ministry takes the standpoint that if God wants us to face the source of our trauma, it will be revealed to us in His timing and when we're prepared to handle it. We've seen people healed without knowledge of their wounding, and we know that growth can occur without full recognition of our past issues.

Most of the time, just the knowledge that our behaviors have a source will restart the growing process. Denial blocks the growing process. The mind needs to understand that there's a reason, not an excuse.

Express pain with a trustworthy person in a safe environment. A little child trusts everyone. We trusted and were badly wounded. In our healing and growth, we learn we have the right to demand that people in our lives earn our trust. We're valuable enough that each person who comes into our lives should prove to be trustworthy.

After being hurt repeatedly, we're afraid of others' ulterior motives. "What do they really want from me?" we ask. We must learn that we're worthy of validation and love.

Right now I want to give you permission to recognize that you're so valuable you have a right to try to understand people's motives. You don't have to trust. It's an adult move to decide whom to trust and from whom to guard your heart. Let others earn your trust and confidence. Time is our best friend when it comes to creating trust in relationships.

Growing intimacy within the bonds of friendship is necessary to replace the missing trust and validation. You'll find trust in friendships with people who can mentor you, who understand what it's like to be wounded, and who will always be a few steps ahead of you on the journey to whole living.

We need mentors and friends who will tell us the truth. We need the body of Christ and a ministry to tell us the truth. Many times when the pastor preaches the truth and identifies our pet sins, we get angry and accuse him or her of meddling. But this is precisely what we need to become teachable people.

Look for unresolved feelings and needs which have been hidden by our pain. Paul wrote in Rom. 8:26, "In the same way, the Spirit helps us in our weakness. We do not know what we ought to pray for, but the Spirit himself intercedes for us with groans that words cannot express."

Paul was a human example of an angry, immature man who didn't know what he truly needed. Even after God stopped him on the road to Damascus, Paul struggled with his relationships and with his calling. For three years he constantly sought truth and growth in his own life before he started his ministry.

He saw himself clearly, in the right perspective as revealed in Phil. 3:12-14: "Not that I have already obtained all this, or have already been made perfect, but I press on to take hold of that for which Christ Jesus took hold of me. Brothers, I do not consider myself yet to have taken hold of it. But one thing I do: Forgetting what is behind and straining toward what is ahead, I press on toward the goal to win the prize for which God has called me heavenward in Christ Jesus."

When we begin to uncover the truth about ourselves, we can start asking real questions about what we need in our lives. We can learn to talk about what we want and need. Everyone communicates differently, and each of us will discover the right method of expressing our needs to those we love. We must take courageous steps to share what's in our hearts and minds. This is the beginning of the journey to wholeness.

Learn to take responsibility for your reactive behavior. Laura Schlessinger writes about freedom and responsibility in her book *The Ten Commandments*. She points out that the flip side of the freedom coin is responsibility. Without responsibility, we could not have true freedom.

We have worked up enough courage to identify our behavior, and possibly even the wounds that caused our actions. Now we must claim responsibility. Part of identifying our reactive behavior means we reach a point at which we can take responsibility for our actions. This may include identifying our sin. God has given us the choice of what to do with our lives and provided His Son as a model. This is key in leading mature lives, making adult decisions, and being involved in loving relationships.

When we tie it all together, our bodies eventually relax. We're all searching for that internal "sigh," the one that finally says, "This all makes sense now." Indeed, the truth really does set us free.

Receive validation and permission to grow and mature. The cycle of a single wounded life was broken in my son Jeff's life when he took his own son aside and said, "Son, there's nothing you can tell me that happened to you, nothing you could say that would cause me not to love you. You will always have my support. Your mom and I will always support you. If somebody hurts you, if somebody touches you inappropriately, if somebody does something to you, you let me know, because I'll be your protector. You always deserve to feel safe and know how much we love you and how valuable and cherished you are to us. Whatever happens, we're going to work it out together."

When Jeff's son came to him and told him that someone had touched him inappropriately, they worked it out. The safety of the home remained intact. My grandson's value remained important and whole. This wholeness is available for us at any stage of life.

STATEMENT OF VALIDATION FOR YOU

I want you to know that nothing you can tell me has happened to you, nothing you could say would cause me not to love you. You will always have my support. You are valuable and beautiful in God's eyes and in my eyes. Nothing has happened or will happen to change that. If someone hurt you before puberty, you can let go of the responsibility of that event. It wasn't your fault, and you couldn't have done anything to prevent it. You deserve to feel safe and know how much you are loved and how valuable you are in God's eyes. I give you permission to grow and mature. I give you permission to become the whole, healthy adult God intends for you to be, capable of emotional bonding and loving, in an abuse-free relationship.

With that statement, I'm telling you that you have permission to release the feelings of shame. The real guilt is God's way of dealing with your wrong behavior. Now your conscience can be trusted as you grow. Guilt signifies that our actions are wrong, but it leaves our core person intact to become a whole, mature child of God. Shame makes us feel as if we're bad to the core—hopeless, "born this way," and frustrated. God has no desire for us to live locked in the shame trap.

Ending the Cycle

Like Jeff and his children, we must prevent the cycle of abuse, silence, and behavior from being repeated in our families. Don't be afraid to talk if a traumatic situation has occurred. Our children should feel they can tell us anything. When they make themselves vulnerable, we must protect their openness. If we're shocked or dismayed and can't communicate, our child will feel rejected and damaged once again by our response.

When we respond in a loving manner and continue to affirm the person's value, we lay the foundation for safety in their lives. In listening to them this way, we're laying down the principles of God's kingdom for unconditional love.

Release the Responsibility of Trauma

In my work, I've encountered many people seeking resolution of a parent's death. They "lost" their mother or father while they were still very young. The adults in their lives wanted to shield them from the pain and reality of death. As a result, the absence of their parents was never fully explained, and they may think from a child's viewpoint that they did something to cause their parent to leave. Such people ask,

- "Why did my mother [father] leave me?"
- "What did I do?"
- "How can I bring her [him] back?"
- "How can I make this right again?"

If under such conditions we were told, "Mom's [or Dad's] choice was to stay here and be your mother, but death is a part of life. That's the way it happened, but it's not your responsibility. You didn't cause the death," then we would understand that our parent loved us but had to go away. We would be released of the responsibility for that death as we heard the truth from our trusted caregivers. In the same way, if we've taken responsibility for any situation in which we were abused, we must release that shame as well. We must understand that we could not prevent our wound and we are not at fault, although we're responsible for our adult reactive behavior.

In all stages of our lives, we need trusted caregivers who can walk with us through this process. We need parents who will give us the truth, and we must be parents who give truth to our children. They can help us take responsibility for our actions and choices after our wounding, giving us the freedom to release the responsibility of the trauma, which we had no means to prevent.

Filling the Empty Spaces

"Come out from them and be separate, says the Lord. Touch no unclean thing, and I will receive you. I will be a Father to you, and you will be my sons and daughters, says the Lord Almighty" (2 Cor. 6:17-18).

Many of us need to finish our fathering. Women have husbands who are not true husbands—not because they're bad men, but because they've never learned how to be husbands. Husbands have wives who are not true wives, not because they're terrible women, but because they've never learned how to be wives.

God designed the Body of Christ to help bring people into a relationship with Him, offering us a model for surrogacy. The greatest surrogacy is that Christ died on the Cross for us that we may live fully and don't have to pay the price for our own sin.

Your life is valuable in God's eyes. Look at the truth about yourself, because you're so important. Don't lead a half-life. Be whole! God wants you to live life to the fullest.

Our software, the programming of our brain, has desperately needed to hear that truth for a lifetime. When we have the right pieces, we can know we're not flawed. We're not deficient.

The Rewiring

As we choose to start the process of recovery and healing, our choice creates new pathways in the brain. Yes, it can be uncomfortable, but it's rewarding. The Scripture tells us to renew our mind on a daily basis. After about 30 to 36 months, we'll see that the choices we made at the beginning of the process are becoming second nature. Then we'll see that we have been given the miracle we have sought.

Several years ago I was asked to create a documentary video on domestic violence. At one point, the director of the video asked me to push and hit Judy—just play-acting—for the tape. I raised my hand to pretend to hit her and felt intensely nauseous. My insides seemed to have turned to water. I could not, even for television, raise my hand against her. When I started my healing process and came back to serve Christ, I said I would die before I treated any woman the way I did in the past.

I was thrilled that I couldn't even act as though I were hitting Judy. It proved to me that what God has revealed in His Word is indeed true and practical: our minds can become rewired to accept new life commandments. The old ways, years and years of battering, have disappeared, and the new ways have become my new nature.

We have to work, with the help of God and our counselors, to reprogram the life commandments that have been imbedded in our wiring. We must let the new directions take root. This permits us to see our value, become stable, to grow, to mature, and to gain control of our lives.

The Rebirth

Jesus says to come to Him as a child. If you're trusting, lowly, humble, and forgiving, you will grow and mature. The process is slow. The mind will do its work. The truth will set you free.

Alan Wright offers this image in his book *A Childlike Heart*: "Don't miss the symbol that Jesus painted for Nicodemus. An old man becoming a tiny baby. Imagine it. Wrinkled skin, blotched by years of hot Judean sun and weathered by arid, Mid-eastern winds, becoming soft, pink, and unblemished. . . . Sagging muscles, brittle bones, and stiff joints transformed into the nimble, elastic anatomy of a toddler. That's how dramatic the change is that Jesus offers" (249).

I can't help but see myself in that picture. I was the biggest jerk on earth for so many years. But, as this book has portrayed, Jesus changed my life radically.

I hope you're convinced. This radical change is what we need for overcoming our life of pain, masks, and unexplainable reactive behavior. Facing the truth and confronting our wounds will bring a change that will alter every aspect of our lives. Our relationships will be fulfilling, our careers will have direction, and our needs and desires will be attainable. Most important, as we grow and mature, we'll be able to develop the character of Christ and live a whole life in His Spirit as it was meant to be lived.

WORKS CITED AND FOR FURTHER READING

Chapter 2

Albers, Robert H. *Shame: A Faith Perspective.* New York: Haworth Pastoral Press, 1995.

Chalmers, Elden M. Personal interviews. Bismarck, N.D., February 1993.

Erickson, Erik H. *Childhood and Society.* New York and London: W. W. Norton and Co., 1963.

Malsakis, Aphrodite. *When the Bough Breaks.* Oakland, Calif.: New Harbinger Publications, 1991.

Moz, Jane Middleton. *Shame and Guilt: Masters of Disguise.* Deerfield Beach, Fla.: Health Communications, 1990.

Chapter 3

Amen, Daniel G. *Change Your Brain, Change Your Life.* New York: Three Rivers Press, 1998.

Bell, Roselyn. *The Hadassah Magazine Jewish Parenting Book.* New York: The Free Press, 1989.

Brand, Paul, and Philip Yancy. *In His Image.* Grand Rapids: Zondervan Publishing House, 1984.

Greenspan, Stanley I., and Beryl Lieff Benderly. *The Growth of the Mind.* Reading, Mass.: Addison-Wesley Publishing Company, 1997.

Hertzberb, Arthur. *Judaism.* New York: Simon and Schuster/Touchstone, 1991.

Hill, Craig. *Bar Barakah.* Littleton, Colo.: Family Foundations International, 1998.

Jensen, Eric. *Teaching with the Brain in Mind.* Alexandria, Va.: Association for Supervision and Curriculum Development, 1998.

Kotulac, Ronald. *Inside the Brain.* Kansas City: Andrews McMeel Publishing, 1996.

Siegel, Daniel J. *The Developing Mind.* New York: Guilford Press; 1999.

Spreen, Otfried, Anthony T. Risser, and Dorothy Edgell. *Developmental Neuropsychology.* New York: Oxford University Press, 1995.

Strassfeld, Sharon, and Kathy Green. *The Jewish Family Book.* New York: Bantam Books, 1981.

van der Kolk, Bessel A., Alexander C. McFarlane, and Lars Weisaeth. *Traumatic Stress.* New York: Guilford Press, 1996.

Chapter 4

Verny, Thomas, and Pamela Weintraub. *Nurturing the Unborn Child.* New York: Bantam Doubleday Dell Publishing Group, 1991.

Chapter 5

Carter, William Lee. *The Angry Teenager.* Nashville: Thomas Nelson Publishers, 1995.

Elkind, David. *All Grown Up and No Place to Go.* Reading, Mass.: Addison Wesley Longman, 1998.

Larson, Scott. *At Risk.* Loveland, Colo.: Group Publishing, 1999.

LeCroy, Craig Winston. *Handbook of Child and Adolescent Treatment Manuals.* New York: Lexington Books, 1994.

Ortlund, Anne. *Children Are Wet Cement.* Fleming H. Revell Co., 1981.

Parrott III, Les. *Helping the Struggling Adolescent.* Grand Rapids: Zondervan Publishing House, 1993.

Rosemund, John. *Teen Proofing.* Kansas City: Andrews McMeel Publishing, 1998.

Sameroff, Arnold J., and Robert N. Emde. *Relationship Disturbances in Early Childhood.* New York: Basic Books, a Division of Harper Collins Publishers, 1989.

Tobias, Cynthia Ulrich. *The Way They Learn.* Colorado Springs, Colo.: Focus on the Family, 1994.

Chapter 6

Kuzma, Kay. *When You're Serious About Love.* Nashville: Thomas Nelson Publishers, 1993.

Sinring, Sue Klavans, Steven S. Simring, and William Proctor. *The Compatability Quotient.* New York: Fawcett Columbine, 1990.

Chapter 7

Gootnick, Irwin. *Why You Behave in Ways You Hate.* Granite Bay, Calif.: 1997.

Gray, John. *What You Feel You Can Heal.* Mill Valley, Calif.: Heart Publishing, 1994.

Truman, Karol K. *Feelings Buried Alive Never Die.* Las Vegas, Nev.: 1991.

Wardle, Terry. *Wounded.* Camp Hill, Pa.: Christian Publications, 1994.

Chapter 8

Dimock, Peter T. *Adults Molested as Children: A Survivor's Manual for Women and Men.* Orwell, Vt.: Safer Society Press, 1988.

Sperling, Michael B., and William H. Berman. *Attachment in Adults.* New York: Guilford Press, 1994.

Thomas, Gary. *Sacred Marriage.* Grand Rapids: Zondervan Publishing House, 2000.

Whitefield, Charles L. *Memory and Abuse.* Deerfield, Fla.: Health Communication, 1995.

Wright, H. Norman. *Making Peace with Your Past.* Grand Rapids: Fleming H. Revell, 1985.

Chapter 9

Bloom, Martin. *Life Span Development: Bases for Prevention and Interventive Helping.* New York: Macmillan Publishing Co., 1980.

Bowling, John C. *Grace-Full Leadership.* Kansas City: Beacon Hill Press of Kansas City, 2000.

Hess, Karol, and Doug McCulley. *Maturity Is a Choice.* Joplin, Mo.: College Press Publishing Co., 1994.

Stockman, Larry V., and Cynthia S. Graves. *Grown-up Children Who Won't Grow Up.* Rocklin, Calif.: Prima Publishing, 1994.

Chapter 10

Brandt, Frans M. J.. *The Renewed Mind.* Enumclaw, Wash.: Wine Press Publishing, 1999.

Flannigan, Beverly. *Forgiving the Unforgivable.* New York: Macmillan Publishing Co., 1992.

Ghezzi, Bert. *Becoming More Like Jesus.* Huntington, Ind.: Our Sunday Visitor Publishing Division, 1987.

Manning, Brennan. *Abba's Child.* Colorado Springs, Colo.: NavPress, 1994

McDowell, Josh. *His Image, My Image.* San Bernardino, Calif.: Here's Life Publishers, 1984.

Chapter 11

Gaub, Ken. *Re-Arranging Your Mental Furniture.* Shippersburg, Pa.: Destiny Image Publishers, 2000.

Linn, Matthew, Sheila Fabricant, and Dennis Linn. *Healing the Eight Stages of Life.* Mahwah, N.J.: Paulist Press, 1988.

Schlessinger, Laura. *The Ten Commandments.* New York: HarperCollins, 1999.

Wright, Alan. *A Childlike Heart,* Sisters, Ore: Multnomah Publishers, 2000.

Zohar, Danah. *Rewiring the Corporate Brain.* San Francisco: Berrett-Koehler Publishers, 1997.

ANGRY MEN AND THE WOMEN WHO LOVE THEM
Breaking the Cycle of Physical and Emotional Abuse

BY PAUL HEGSTROM

Paul Hegstrom lived the first 40 years of his life not understanding the driving force that caused him to self-destruct again and again. A failed, violent marriage, a second, more violent relationship, $20,000 worth of therapy—and still the rage continued. Violence, drugs, and alcohol became a way of life until a long-term jail sentence convinced him that he needed help. Facing severe consequences, Paul was motivated to discover the root of his problems and turn completely toward Christ.

The dramatic change in his life led Paul to take steps to help other families in jeopardy. Thousands of hours of research and facilitating domestic violence groups for women and developing a teen program led to the establishment of the Life Skills International program. Paul and his wife, Judy, remarried in 1983, and their second marriage is free from abuse.

Angry Men and the Women Who Love Them is based on Paul's life and work. For the man who batters, the woman who feels trapped, and the pastor, counselor, or friend who desperately wants to help them both, *Angry Men and the Women Who Love Them* offers straight, biblical answers for those who are willing to make tough decisions and overcome the cycle of violence.

Angry Men and the Women Who Love Them
ISBN 083-411-6766
Order toll-free from **Beacon Hill Press of Kansas City**
800-877-0700